SPECIAL
EDUCATIONAL
NEEDS IN THE
EARLY YEARS

SPECIAL EDUCATIONAL NEEDS IN THE EARLY YEARS

A Guide to Inclusive Practice

PENNY BORKETT

Los Angeles | London | New Delhi
Singapore | Washington DC | Melbourne

Los Angeles | London | New Delhi
Singapore | Washington DC | Melbourne

SAGE Publications Ltd
1 Oliver's Yard
55 City Road
London EC1Y 1SP

SAGE Publications Inc.
2455 Teller Road
Thousand Oaks, California 91320

SAGE Publications India Pvt Ltd
B 1/I 1 Mohan Cooperative Industrial Area
Mathura Road
New Delhi 110 044

SAGE Publications Asia-Pacific Pte Ltd
3 Church Street
#10-04 Samsung Hub
Singapore 049483

Editor: Delayna Spencer
Editorial assistant/Senior assistant editor: Orsod Malik/Catriona McMullen
Production editor: Nicola Carrier
Copyeditor: Jane Fricker
Proofreader: Leigh C. Smithson
Indexer: Silvia Benvenuto
Marketing manager: Lorna Patkai
Cover design: Wendy Scott
Typeset by: C&M Digitals (P) Ltd, Chennai, India
Printed in the UK

Library of Congress Control Number: 2019955942

British Library Cataloguing in Publication data

A catalogue record for this book is available from the British Library

ISBN 978-1-5264-6736-2
ISBN 978-1-5264-6735-5 (pbk)

At SAGE we take sustainability seriously. Most of our products are printed in the UK using responsibly sourced papers and boards. When we print overseas we ensure sustainable papers are used as measured by the PREPS grading system. We undertake an annual audit to monitor our sustainability.

CONTENTS

ABOUT THE AUTHOR

Penny Borkett is Senior Lecturer in Early Years and Early Childhood Studies at Sheffield Hallam University, UK. During her working life she has worked as a teaching assistant, Portage worker, Special Educational Needs Co-ordinator and Integrated Services Co-ordinator for a Sure Start children's centre. She then joined academia and this is her second book.

Penny has always been passionate about inclusion, especially when focusing on children with special educational needs and disabilities. So this book brings together much of her life's work in supporting children and their families.

ACKNOWLEDGEMENTS

I have so many to thank for the writing of this book. The people listed here are the students, practitioners, parents and lecturers who have supported me through the long and at times difficult process of writing this book. Many thanks to you all. Recognition also needs to be made of the many children and their families who I have worked with over the past 30 years. Not only did you have an impact on my work but you helped to shape the person that I have become – thank you.

Students on the Foundation Degree in Early Years 2018 at Sheffield Hallam University

Norfolk Park School, especially to Matt Cam and Lindsay Newbould

Granby Nursery chain, especially Jo Gray and Jacqui Hannaby

Sue and John Freeman

Lynne Brierley-Barber

Sharon Smith

Bibiana Wigley

Eleanor, Michael and Graham Borkett

Julie and Annabel Drabble

Then there are others too who have supported me. All the children that I have worked with over my 30-year career in early years. Those families I visited whilst I was a Portage worker and all the professionals who I have worked alongside over the years. My children Mary and Hannah, who first inspired in me a love for the youngest children and set me on my long and varied career path in the early years. My grandchildren Evie, Bethany and Oliver, who I love spending time with and who surprise and amaze me all of the time. My endlessly patient husband Phill, who has always believed in me. I thank him for his endless support and patient editing. Delayna Spencer, Catriona McMullen and Orsod Malik from Sage, who have supported me through the writing of the book. Finally, thanks to God for his guidance throughout my life.

I dedicate this book to my Mum, Irene Phillippo, who sadly did not live to see the book in publication.

[R]emember that everyone is a human being. Value every child for who they are. Start with what they can do, not what they can't… Never consider there is an alternative; every child is entitled to a preschool place. (Purdue, 2009: 142)

GLOSSARY

Academy An independent school whose funding comes directly from the government rather than the Local Authority.

Agency Giving a child the opportunity to choose something for themselves. This might be in terms of an activity, snack or who they want to play with.

Amniocentesis test A test carried out during pregnancy to ascertain whether the foetus could have Down syndrome.

Augmentative communication Communication systems such as Makaton, Picture Exchange Communication System, or computer-based communication systems.

Austerity A political term which refers to a period in history where the government has to slash funding, particularly to local authorities and the work that they do in supporting education, health and social care.

Cognition Relates to a child's ability to think, remember, problem solve and make decisions for themselves.

Degenerative An illness that gradually affects someone. The person's health will get worse over time.

Ethnography A method of carrying out research within a particular environment that the researcher has spent a lot of time working or living in.

Eye pointing When a non-verbal child uses their eyes to communicate. They may be given a choice of two activities and look at a particular one as their favoured activity.

Formative Assessment that is informal and is noted on a day-to-day basis. This may be recorded on Post-it notes.

Holistic An approach to learning that emphasises the importance of all areas of development – the physical, cognitive, communicative, emotional and psychological wellbeing of children

Key worker   Somebody who is responsible for a small group of children in an early years setting. They will build a relationship with the child and parent, and be responsible for planning and assessing the children in their care.

Neoliberalism   A term used to describe how public policies are written. It favours competition and is evident in education through the standards-driven system in place in the UK.

New Labour   A dominant political force in the UK from the mid-1990s until 2010, under the leadership of Tony Blair.

Pedagogy   The method and practice of teaching.

Philanthropist   A person who tries to do good and seeks to improve the welfare of others often by donating large amounts of money.

Rite of passage   A ceremony or event marking an important stage in someone's life which requires a transition of some kind; it might relate to starting school, being married, having a child, for example.

Sociology   The study of the development of society and how this affects certain practices.

Summative   An assessment of learning usually carried out in schools at the end of a period of time which ascertains what the child has learnt.

MULTI-AGENCY ROLES MENTIONED IN THE BOOK

Educational psychologist   A trained psychologist who is employed by the local authority and would become involved with a family if a child is thought to or has a SEND.

Family support worker   Will establish a relationship with individual families, assess their needs, and decide their eligibility for various types of aid, benefits and equipment and support them through the application processes.

Health visitors   These are nurses or midwives who are passionate about promoting healthy lifestyles and preventing illness. They work with families to give pre-school-age children the best possible start in life. They may be the first person to suggest that a child may have a SEND.

Occupational therapist   Provides support to people whose health or development prevents them doing the activities that matter to them.

Paediatrician   A doctor who only works with babies and young children. She or he would take over the care of children if they were born with some kind of SEND.

Physiotherapist   Helps children with physical disabilities. They will often give the child exercises to strengthen or build their muscles.

Portage worker   An early years intervention worker who visits a child and their family when there is thought to be a special educational need or disability.

Social worker   Someone who is responsible for helping children, families, and groups of people to cope with problems they're facing. They may support families in claiming benefits, or finding respite care for children.

Speech and language therapist   Supports children's communication skills and may be involved with a child's swallowing and way they use their mouth.

INTRODUCTION

THE IMPORTANCE OF INCLUSION AND WHY IT IS A THREAD RUNNING THROUGH THIS BOOK

A major focus of this book is inclusion, and I make no apologies for this. Within the British educational system it is recommended that children with special educational needs and disabilities (SEND) should, wherever possible, be educated in mainstream schools. Therefore it is vital that any book that relates to SEND needs to embed that philosophy within it. For this reason the second chapter particularly relates to the importance of inclusion and is situated towards the beginning of the book. For me, inclusion is a vital principle that I have tried to ensure is rooted in each chapter. I do however recognise that for practitioners this can be a tricky issue, which will divide opinion. I was always very aware when I went into lecturing that it was easy for me to teach about inclusion, but often much harder for practitioners to orchestrate it. I hope that as you come to read the book you too can focus on it through the lens of inclusion. If you find it difficult to think favourably about inclusion, maybe because of your own experience or the experiences of others, please try to read it with an open mind.

I think it is also important to recognise that it can become too easy to focus on children whose disabilities are visible: for instance children with Down syndrome, those with hearing difficulties who need to wear aids, children with cerebral palsy whose disability is obvious and who may receive from society a certain amount of pity because of this. There will be many more for whom their disabilities are not visible, whose behaviour may be affected and for whom normal everyday life (which you and I take for granted) can be fraught with difficulties (Boyle et al., 2011). Many of these children may be growing up in areas of deprivation, with families who may not have much knowledge of bringing up children or have not experienced positive parenting themselves. In 2015 the Early Intervention Foundation suggested that children born in deprived areas are more likely to experience emotional issues under the age of three. They suggest that if not dealt with, these experiences can affect them into adolescence and may affect their educational attainment throughout life.

This book relates to all children. The Early Years Foundation Stage (Department for Children, Schools and Families [DCSF], 2008) has continually encouraged practitioners to see all children as unique. Therefore it is important that whilst reading the book you consider all the children who you work with. Most children at some time in their lives will need some extra support. Maybe when a new sibling is born, they move house, someone they love dies or something difficult happens in their lives. Without the right amount of support from encouraging and sensitive practitioners, these experiences can have a major impact on children in many different ways. This book includes tips and ways of working that you may like to use and which could have a positive effect on children who you know or who you work with.

ABOUT THE LAYOUT OF THIS BOOK

At the beginning of the book you will find a glossary. This explains words, concepts or principles mentioned (in the book) which you may not know about. It also includes a list of the many practitioners whose titles you may be aware of but whose roles are new to you. This particularly relates to those professionals who may be involved in a child's or family's life when early intervention may be offered. Hopefully the glossary will support your learning and knowledge as you read through the book.

The chapters flow from one to the next and will take the reader on a journey through some of the vital elements of special educational needs and disability (SEND). Each chapter is divided into three sections, all of which attempt to meet one of three learning outcomes given at the beginning and end of each chapter. The chapters chosen were shaped very much by my own career and aspects that I felt were valuable to share. They are all a mix of theory, policy and practice. This is really important as all aspects of early years provision are sanctioned in history, policy and practice. Many times I have heard students ask 'Why do we need to focus on policy and indeed politics?'. But without understanding the nature of politics and how it has shaped educational history it is hard to understand why and how policies were initially developed and the ways that they are used within practice in the 21st century.

The chapters have a number of reflection points scattered throughout. These encourage the reader to think about something that has been written that needs more consideration. I hope that you will consider these points and draw your own conclusions to the questions raised. The chapters also include case studies. These are all fictional but do relate in some part to the dilemmas and celebrations that I have experienced in my very rich and varied career. They too have reflection points to encourage readers to examine their own views of inclusion and early years practice. If you are a lecturer and reading this book from the perspective of a tutor, please feel free to use the case studies and reflection points as a tool for your teaching.

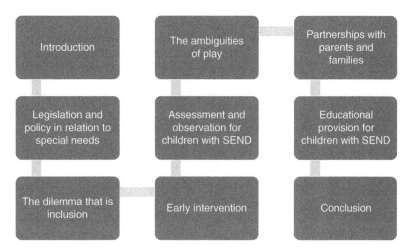

Figure 0.1 The journey of this book for the reader

They also include a personal comment from me. These may relate to things that I have discovered during my career or to ways of working that I could share. These are entirely my views and are available for you to either agree or disagree with. Hopefully these may get you thinking about the benefits and dilemmas of working with children who have SEND or they may suggest new ways of working which you may want to try.

At the end of each chapter there are links to some extra reading. In most cases they include chapters of other books, research articles and details of internet sites. By reading some of them you may learn of different ways of working that might be useful to you.

When writing a book it is important to try and ensure that what is written about is up to date and reflects what is going on in practice over time. In order to ensure that this book is authentic and up to date I have included the views of others in the book. I hope this will ensure that it is an honest account of what goes on in settings day to day.

I have also chosen to refer to the term SEND – children with special educational needs and disabilities – as when the new Code of Practice was launched by the Department for Education and Department for Health this term was introduced. For me this legislative paper uses the term and so I too have chosen to use this from Chapter 2 onwards. It is always hard to distinguish the particular needs of young children and so it seemed more useful to use this term. I have also used the term practitioners throughout the book. This does not distinguish any one particular role in a hierarchical way but instead sees all practitioners as essential in the role of working with children. In the same way, I refer to settings rather than schools/nurseries/pre-schools/childminders; again it is easier to use the one term rather than differentiating them.

I hope that you enjoy reading this book and that my passion for inclusion and working with children with SEND comes through.

Having discussed the background of the book I will now go on to introduce each chapter and to give further detail as to what they each include.

CHAPTER 1 - LEGISLATION AND POLICY IN RELATION TO SPECIAL NEEDS

The historical aspect of policy is important to discuss as it gives the reader an underlying sense of how much education has changed since 1870. In 150 years education has seen huge changes and will continue to do so as governments and societies change and different priorities are adopted.

In the first part of Chapter 1 there is an explanation of why policy is necessary – this is something that is important to recognise as early years practice is constantly evolving and at times quite challenging to keep up with. Alongside this it is important when working with children with SEND to recognise the place of the Special Educational Needs and Disability Code of Practice, which was first written in 2001 and reviewed in 2014. This is the legislative framework that all practitioners should draw on if they have children in their setting with SEND. I have regularly spoken to early years practitioners who have no awareness of this code. Without this document it is hard to know how children and families should be supported. This chapter also discusses how the three main political parties in England – the Conservatives, Labour and Liberal Democrats – view education. This is something which it is important that practitioners understand, as with the many elections held in the UK different parties come into government with differing priorities and standards. Part of the reason why the Early Years Foundation Stage (EYFS) has changed so much is because different governments have been in power from its inception in 2008 to 2019, the time of writing this book.

The chapter then takes the reader on a journey that seeks to introduce how educational policy has evolved over the years. It begins with the 1870 Education Act, which was written to prevent schooling in England from being the responsibility of the church and rich philanthropists and to move to the provision of free education, as something that all children should be entitled to. This part of the chapter also gives a picture of the way that children with SEND were educated around the time of the first Education Act and why in 1978 Mary Warnock was charged with leading a review on SEND. Thankfully, as a result of this it became more common for children with SEND to be educated alongside their peers in mainstream schools. Obviously it would be impossible to discuss all the policies in this book, so there is more of a focus on those which have direct impact on children with SEND.

It is pertinent here to realise that at times international policy can become a catalyst for change. This was the case when two international policies were introduced – these being the United Nations Convention on the Rights of the Child (United Nations International Children's Emergency Fund [UNICEF], 1989) and the Salamanca Statement launched by the United Nations Educational, Scientific and Cultural Organization (UNESCO) in 1994. Here we see international proclamations impacting on educational policy in the UK, particularly in respect to children with SEND. The chapter continues to discuss the evolving nature of the EYFS and the importance of the SEND Code of Practice (DFE and DOH, 2014) in the UK.

CHAPTER 2 - THE DILEMMA THAT IS INCLUSION

The content of this chapter has been placed early in the book because of the importance of inclusion, particularly in the early years. Inclusive practice is something that I am passionate about, especially in relation to children from other cultures and those with SEND. Therefore the book needed to have an inclusive thread running through it. I would have liked this chapter to have been the first in the book, but because inclusion relates so much to legislation and policy it was more appropriate to place it after that chapter.

The chapter begins with some discussion of exclusion. Before discussing issues around inclusion, it is firstly pertinent to consider who in society is excluded. It suggests differing views around exclusion and makes suggestions regarding those who are excluded on a regular basis. It is suggested that those with SEND are often excluded in both covert ways and more overt, obvious ways (Nutbrown et al., 2013). An example of discrimination might be when public schools covertly discriminate against children with SEND as their entry requirements are so rigid that those children with SEND could never be offered a place. An example of discriminating overtly might be a setting that accommodates a number of children in wheelchairs and using walking aids only displays books, pictures and posters representing able-bodied children.

Discussion in the chapter then moves to focus on the evolving nature of inclusion and how it has changed over the years. It makes the suggestion that at times practitioners need to reflect on their own experiences and views of inclusion before they can start to be part of a team that can offer fully inclusive practice. In this section I asked the students I was teaching at the time to come up with their definitions of what inclusion is – they may prove interesting reading. The final section discusses ways in which settings can be more inclusive. It encourages practitioners to focus on all areas of the provision to ensure that it meets the needs of all children. This includes the environment, as for example very bright colours can overstimulate children; and it also encourages practitioners to consider carefully the communication needs of children in the setting.

CHAPTER 3 - EARLY INTERVENTION

Any book focusing on SEND provision in the early years should include a chapter about the effectiveness of early intervention. When I was a Portage worker at the start of the century, early intervention in the main related to very young children who were either born with or suspected to have some degree of SEND. Over the years, research indicated that families living in areas of deprivation were more likely to suffer health and educational inequalities and therefore require support early on in their children's lives. With the instigation of Sure Start programmes in 1999, early intervention was offered to many more children and families living in deprived areas. These centres offered bespoke services that met the individual needs of the community.

The work of Urie Bronfenbrenner and the ecological systems theory is introduced and explained in an attempt to support the reader's understanding of how issues such as poverty, poor housing and bad parenting can affect a child's development and learning. This theory views all aspects of people's lives as interrelated and supports the view that if there are difficulties in one area of a family's life it will have direct impact on others. An example of this might be when a refugee family mother and child are going to a parent and toddler group which costs them a pound a week to attend. The father in the family then loses his job, which means that the mother can no longer afford to attend the group. This could have a detrimental effect on both the mother and the child. The mother will lose her social support network with the parents she has got to know and the child loses their ability to mix with other children and experience the activities which support their development and learning.

The chapter then goes on to introduce some of the early intervention programmes used in England. This is certainly not an exhaustive list, but many of those mentioned are in current use and are an asset to both the children concerned and the families. However, as with many principles in early years practice there are benefits and challenges to these support systems, which the chapter tries to identify. The chapter concludes by discussing the impacts of these on both the children and families concerned.

CHAPTER 4 - ASSESSMENT AND OBSERVATION FOR CHILDREN WITH SPECIAL EDUCATIONAL NEEDS AND DISABILITY

This chapter focuses on the importance of assessment. This is seen by some as being quite controversial, and it raises differing views depending on your own experience and how other professionals view the role of assessment. However, it is something that needs to be addressed as it holds such a prominent position when addressing the needs of children with SEND.

The chapter begins by offering some suggestions as to what assessment is and the different ways that it is used by practitioners in settings. It goes on to explain how it is linked to curricula, particularly focusing on the EYFS. It then discusses changes that are currently being made by the Department for Education in order to support children with SEND whose needs are not currently being met by the National Curriculum, and goes on to introduce new ways of working that will hopefully support children in a more effective way.

It also discusses changes that the Office for Standards in Education, Children's Services and Skills (Ofsted) have made in light of their recent reviews and their newly revised equality statement. The statement encourages leaders and managers to work with their teams to ensure that all children are allowed equality of opportunity wherever they go to school.

The second section focuses particularly on two important documents – the EYFS and the SEND Code of Practice – and what these documents say about the role of assessment. It introduces two levels of SEND support for children and discusses the part that local authorities should play in ascertaining the correct provision for children and their families. It also discusses some of the challenges local authorities are currently experiencing in terms of services available to children with SEND.

The final section of the chapter discusses how practitioners may record the development and learning of children through observations, and also focuses on the importance of including the voice of the child in assessments. Again this is a controversial area of practice as it can be difficult for children with SEND to voice their views. However, with the use of different communication aids and methodologies, children with SEND should be able to have a voice in decisions that affect them.

CHAPTER 5 - THE AMBIGUITIES OF PLAY

This was (in my view) an important principle to discuss in this book. For many years I have been on the receiving end of comments from practitioners and parents alike bemoaning the fact that children with SEND play differently from other children. I sometimes wondered whether there was some kind of 'golden rule' that dictates how it is that children should play. It is important to acknowledge that in the West, play is seen as the panacea for learning. This is in contrast to many other cultures which view play as being something that is done at the end of the day, after school and when all the chores have been done (Borkett, 2018). Despite all of this I wanted to try and address why it is that some children with SEND do struggle with play.

The chapter therefore begins by discussing why in the West play and development are intrinsically linked. There is discussion around the standards-driven educational system that the current government extols, and how this can hinder a play-based curriculum which is so important to children. The chapter then goes on to explore what play is – you may think this is quite a strange concept to try to explain, but once you start to read the chapter you will see that there are very many different views on the purpose of play. This therefore makes it hard to quantify, and to explain to those who do not see its significance to children's development and learning.

The chapter discusses many of the theorists who wrote, or who currently write, about the development of young children and how they explore, develop and learn. The theorists considered are Froebel, whose work began in the 18th century, Montessori, Vygotsky, Goldschmied and Bruner, whose work evolved in the 19th century, and the more recent work of Barbara Rogoff in the 21st century. These theories are described and evaluated in terms of how they relate to children with SEND.

The final section of this chapter spends time considering the vital role of the practitioner in facilitating and encouraging children to learn through the medium of play. It is so important that play can be broken down into tiny steps and that practitioners understand their part in supporting play. This is even more important when considering the needs of children with SEND. The chapter goes on to discuss some of the skills that practitioners need in both setting out environments for learning and when interacting with young children. At times they will need to intercede and model kinds of play, but at other times it will be vital to sit back and watch how the child is able to play independently and to observe how they use certain resources. Finally the chapter discusses certain types of play that are important for all children.

CHAPTER 6 - PARTNERSHIPS WITH PARENTS AND FAMILIES

This chapter begins by looking at some of the historical changes that have emerged over the years, relating to working with parents. These have changed massively over the past 100 years and they firmly impact on the way that practitioners work in the here and now. It is also important to address how the support given to families of children with SEND has changed thankfully over the years.

It then moves on to discuss the agonising process that parents go through when they are given the label of a child's disability or when they suspect that their child's development is delayed. This is another chapter where the views of others have been sought. Two parents and a practitioner discussed their journeys and shared some important challenges which are further discussed in the chapter. I have also noted in some detail the grief that some parents go through when a diagnosis is made. Over the years I have been saddened by the views of practitioners that if only parents could accept their child's disability then it would be better for everyone. This section relates to that grief process and the fact that this is something that parents visit time and time again in their child's life. When every rite of passage comes along for their child, so again does the grief.

The chapter focuses very much on the importance of teamwork and how practitioners should work together sensitively, collectively and consistently to support families. The parents involved related to services that can be fragmented and hard to manoeuvre their way around, and some felt that their views were not heard.

The final section of the chapter focuses on the role of the family and how it has changed in the past 50 years. The fact that it is now not uncommon for children to be brought up by parents of the same gender, in blended families where new relationships have been forged and in single-parent families is discussed. This in itself can affect society and has an impact on policy too. So it is important to discuss the effect this can have on practitioners working with parents and families every day. The chapter also discusses how other members of a family may be affected by a sibling who has SEND.

CHAPTER 7 - EDUCATIONAL PROVISION FOR CHILDREN WITH SPECIAL EDUCATIONAL NEEDS AND DISABILITY

This chapter firstly discusses how policy and legislation have evolved over the years in order to give parents the choices of different educational provision if their child has a SEND. It discusses how, since Mary Warnock reviewed education in the UK, mainstream schools have opened their doors more to children with SEND and the impact that this may have on other children in the settings. It sets out differences between the medical and social model of disabilities and the impact this has on education in the UK.

The second section focuses on the benefits and challenges of educating children with SEND in mainstream settings, or in enhanced resource units whereby they are educated in a separate building or room for part of the day and then go into mainstream classes for the remainder of the time.

The final section of this chapter relates to the role of special schools and inclusion. It is quite a controversial suggestion that special schools can be inclusive. However, it is my view that because of the wide-ranging difficulties that children in special schools have, bespoke packages of support are needed that assist all elements of a child's development and learning. Again the views of practitioners have been included in this chapter.

CHAPTER 8 - CONCLUSION

The closing chapter will draw together and make concluding comments on all of the chapters in this book. It will also discuss some of the conclusions that I have drawn whilst working on this book.

I hope that you will find the book useful and that it will have an impact on your knowledge and practice and in the work that you do now and in the future.

1

LEGISLATION AND POLICY IN RELATION TO SPECIAL NEEDS

This chapter will focus on some of the many legal aspects of SEND and how policies support the work that is done in settings when children are thought to or do have SEND.

By the end of this chapter you will:

- understand why legislation and policy are a fundamental part of education practice

- be aware of how policy relating to special needs was first introduced and how it developed both internationally and nationally during the 20th century

- consider how policy has changed during the early years of the 21st century and the implications of this for families and children with SEND.

This chapter will begin by considering why legislation and policy are so important in education, and will continue to discuss the evolving purpose of policy and why it has changed during particular periods of history. Armstrong suggested in 2002 that the planning of policy making can sometimes seem 'fragmented' (p. 446), with various political parties wanting different outcomes. Further discussion will offer the view that in the main, policy may relate to power and, in the case of this book, power over children who have special educational needs and disabilities (SEND). Beland et al. state:

> Throughout the last couple of decades, academics have increasingly emphasized the importance of political ideas in understanding processes of change and stability in politics. (2016: 315)

The second part of the chapter will go on to examine how education policies were established and orchestrated to meet the needs of children with SEND during the 20th century. It will take a journey through the structure of some international and national policies and will focus on the historic reasoning around the formation of these. The groundbreaking work of Mary Warnock will be introduced, discussing how she and her committee instigated some of the first steps into inclusion as we know it.

The final section of the chapter will discuss how policy has changed more recently in the beginning of the 21st century. It will introduce the purpose of the Special Educational Needs (SEN) Code of Practice introduced in 2001, and the changes this has gone through more recently in the redrafting of the 2014 Special Educational Needs and Disability (SEND) Code of Practice.

THE PURPOSE OF POLICY

Firstly, it is worth considering why policies are needed to support practice. Levin (1997) suggests that policies guide and shape practice – the evolving nature of the early years curriculum is an example of this. As new governments are elected, changes are often made to existing priorities depending on the political bias of the government in power.

Policies can introduce new actions needed because of changes in society – an example of this was the need to rewrite the SEN Code of Practice which was first introduced in 2001 by the then New Labour government (Department for Education and Skills [DFES], 2001b). Carpenter (2005) postulates that during this time politically the United Kingdom was 'ripe for the development of a nationally cohesive approach' to children with SEN (p. 176), particularly on reflection of figures suggested by the Office of National Statistics that one in five children had some kind of special educational need (Melzer et al., 2000). Levin (1997) makes the suggestion that when policies are written they usually:

- bring together of a group of people – these may be a government department, a local authority, or an individual setting
- relate to a course of action – in this case actions around children with SEND
- are specific to a way of dealing with particular issues.

REFLECTION

Consider some of the policies that you use in your everyday work or that you are aware of.

- Do they discuss particular groups of children?

- Do they relate to particular actions that may need to be taken in certain circumstances?

- Do they suggest particular ways of doing things or actions that need to be taken in practice?

POLITICAL VIEWS OF EDUCATION

At this point it is useful to consider what the current educational priorities are for particular governments. Current policies favoured by the Conservative government relate to free schools which are funded by the state but run by parents, teachers, or other outside organisations. They support the academies, which were introduced in 2010 by the then Conservative and Liberal Democratic Coalition government. They also believe in a 'target driven' education process which relates to standards rather than the process of education, placing emphasis on literacy and numeracy (Dickens, 2017).

In contrast, the Labour Party would like to see children in school being looked after from 8.00am until 6.00pm to support parents who are working. They would increase spending on education in line with inflation and cap class sizes to 30.

The Liberal Democrat Party see education as a life-long pursuit that enables 'self-fulfilment' (2017: 1) and an enrichment of people's lives. They would like to restructure schools according to the needs of communities and to give greater support for schools in areas of disadvantage.

Interestingly, when the Conservative and Liberal Democrat Coalition government led by David Cameron and Nick Clegg was in power, they introduced the pupil premium for children who may be vulnerable or have particular needs and require extra support with education (Wilkinson, 2015: 18). This remains today despite the fact that the Coalition government is no longer in power. The Liberal Democrats also believe that schools within communities should share resources – this might suggest that staff from special schools could be involved in training around inclusion with mainstream schools (Avramidis et al., 2000).

LEVELS OF POLICY MAKING

Policy in relation to children with SEN often comes in three tiers:

- International/European recommendations, guidelines or statements – these could include the United Nations Convention on the Rights of the Child (UNCRC) (UNICEF, 1989) and the Salamanca Statement (UNESCO, 1994)
- National policies, which include the Special Educational Needs Code of Practice (DFES, 2001) and the Children and Families Act 2014
- Local policies – these may be drawn up by local authorities which are then adopted by all settings in an area. They also relate to individual policies that you may have in your setting.

Baldock et al. (2013) suggest that policies usually originate from people in charge, such as international organisations, governments and local authorities. Rix et al. (2013) postulate that there are many legislative and international agreements that have been drawn up across the world that have transformed mainstream education and special provision.

Through the process and many phases of policy development they go out to consultation, and you may well have contributed to one of these discussions. Recently it has become popular for such discussions to be available through social media platforms, thereby opening up the discussion more widely to parents and practitioners (Sunstein, 2017). This is a positive step because it gives people who may never have considered having a say about government policy to make their views known.

REFLECTION ————————————————

- Why is it important that policies should be open to consultation?

- Have you ever responded to a consultation relating to a particular policy, and why did you feel it important to do so?

- Do you feel that it is your place to respond to consultations relating to Early Years or SEND provision?

PERSONAL NOTE 1.1 ———————————————

During the 2000s I was working as a Special Educational Needs Co-ordinator (SENCO) in a Sure Start centre. In the area there was a high proportion of children with SEND. One of the first things that I had to do was write policies relating to the way that families and children were supported through activities offered in the centre. During this time I was also studying for an MA in Inclusive Education. Although I had experience of working in a special school, I believed vehemently that very young children with special needs should be offered an inclusive education in a mainstream setting.

However one of the activities that the local authority ran was a playgroup for children with SEND which went on within the vicinity of the centre. The plan was for staff from the centre to take over and run the playgroup. I did not see this as 'inclusive' education. I had many discussions with Portage workers, educational psychologists, physiotherapists, health visitors and parents alike. Gradually I realised that although these children were being segregated during their time at the play-group, these sessions did prepare the children for activities and ways of learning that would support their later educational experience in mainstream school.

Consider

- What are your own personal views about this case study – do you view the situation as being inclusive and if so, why?
- Is it acceptable for children with SEND to be involved in similar groups?
- How does your setting help to support children with SEND who may be preparing to go into mainstream education?

Having focused on the role of policy and the impact it has on certain areas of practice, discussion will move on to explain how policy established the role of schools in the 20th century.

EDUCATION IN THE 20TH CENTURY

The 1870 Education Act was established by the Liberal government in order to build more schools and to move away from the reliance of them being established by religious organisations. Around the same time the National Education League began to campaign for free compulsory, non-religious education for all children. The philanthropists involved in setting up schools believed that education was vital to the country as it would enable children to move into manufacturing at the end of their time in school.

In 1918 the Education Act:

- raised the school-leaving age from 12 to 15
- widened the provision of nursery schools and special education
- transferred funding for schools from local authorities to central government
- introduced more professionalism in the workforce by allowing teachers salaries and pensions (www.parliament.uk).

It also became compulsory for children with disabilities to attend school. In the period from 1921 to 1950, so-called 'institutions' were introduced for those with visual or hearing impairments, physical disabilities, breathing difficulties and epilepsy. The view during this time was that it was important that children with disabilities should be educated away from their homes and in residential schools, with a very small number being educated in mainstream settings. Some of these special schools were funded through charities such as the Royal National Institute for the Blind (RNIB). Tomlinson suggests that:

> education systems do not develop spontaneously or in an evolutionary manner. They develop because it is in the interest of particular groups in society that they should develop in specific ways. (1982: 43)

This might suggest that such philanthropists and charities may have wanted to promote their own interests by providing education for those who were seen as being 'vulnerable'. This goes along with the view of Armstrong that reflects a 'humanitarian' account of the growth of special education which was concerned with 'doing good to disabled children' (2002: 441).

Historic England (n.d.) make the suggestion that whilst it was important that all children with SEND were educated, the reality was that children were being taught by low-skilled practitioners and their education was more akin to low-skilled work training. As well as this, parents were not encouraged to visit the schools. This may have been because of the harsh discipline practices that were exerted inside these institutions.

EDUCATION ACT 1944

In 1944 a new Education Act was passed which focused more on secondary education. Children with SEND continued to be categorised according to their disability. Many children in the country were seen as being 'educationally sub-normal' or 'maladjusted' and they too continued to be educated in special schools (Borsay, 2012).

These older views on the education of children with SEND very much relate to the medical model of disability. This in turn relates to the medical needs of the child and makes the assumption that the child/person needs 'fixing'. There will be more discussion around this in Chapter 7, where educational provision for children is discussed.

THE WARNOCK REVIEW

In 1978 an academic called Mary Warnock was tasked by the then Conservative Party Secretary of Education, Margaret Thatcher, to carry out a review into the education of children with SEND. Through this important and groundbreaking work, Warnock and her committee suggested that all previous words linked to disability should be abolished and that the term Special Educational Needs should be used when discussing disability. This was seen at the time as a progressive move by proponents such as Corbett (1996), who believed that this was a much needed action.

Through the Warnock Review mainstream education became a right for all children. However, there was some criticism of those involved with the review. The committee was primarily composed of academics with only one parent and one person with SEND included. Barton and Landman (1993) comment that the committee, rather than observing practice going on in schools, should also have talked to children being educated within these institutions about their experiences. Rather than viewing mainstream as an area of human rights, it was instead being shaped by so-called 'experts within education' who had little experience of special provision. They conclude that the review, rather than being about social justice and equality, was more widely about resources and facilities.

Other changes brought about by the Warnock Review were:

- statements of Special Educational Needs should be established which clearly set out and define the needs of the child and what they would need access to before joining education
- support for children in the early years who may have a SEND or are not developing at the same rate as their peers
- closer working relationships were needed between the agencies working with children
- targets for all children should be based upon 'common educational goals' for all, regardless of their abilities.

This new approach to education continued through the 1990s and began a move away from special schools as parents chose for their children to be educated in mainstream. It was also responsible for greater numbers of children being diagnosed with SEND. As well as national policies relating to SEND there was, at this time, growing international pressure for children with SEND to be educated in mainstream schools.

During this time in English history the social model of disability was emerging. This model, rather than focusing on 'what is wrong with the child', focuses more on how society treats and disables children with SEND. This more positive and inclusive approach relates very much to the work of Warnock and her beliefs that children with SEND should be educated in mainstream schools. As with the medical model of disability, there will more discussion of this in Chapter 7.

INTERNATIONAL STATEMENTS AND GUIDANCE RELATING TO SPECIAL EDUCATIONAL NEEDS

UNITED NATIONS CONVENTION ON THE RIGHTS OF THE CHILD (UNCRC)

In 1989 the United Nations International Children's Emergency Fund (UNICEF) produced the first legally binding international agreement setting out the civil, political, economic, social and cultural rights of children. To date 194 countries have signed up to it and they are bound by international law to ensure that it is implemented. The Convention sets out 54 articles relating to all areas of a child's life. It explains how governments and adults should work collaboratively to ensure that all children have their own rights. Those particularly related to children who have SEND are:

Article 1 – The convention applies to **all children** without discrimination – whatever their ethnicity, religion, language, gender or any other status.

Article 12 – **Every child** has a right to express their views on issues that affect them.

Article 15 – **Every child** has the right to meet with other children and to join groups and organisations.

Article 23 – A child with a disability has the right to **live a full life with dignity** and independence and to play an active part in their community.

Article 28 – **Every child** has a right to an education which should be free.

Article 29 – Education must develop **every child's** personality, talents and abilities.

Article 30 – **Every child** has the right to relax, play and take part in cultural and artistic activities.

The Convention has considerably changed how children are thought of. Before the statement, children were seen as being vulnerable and silent. The Convention has changed the status of a child to being someone with a voice and an entitlement to have a say in all matters that affect them (Borkett, 2019).

THE SALAMANCA STATEMENT

The Centre for Studies on Inclusive Education (CSIE) describe how, in 1994, 92 representatives from governments and organisations across the international community met in Salamanca, Spain, in order to endorse the practice of inclusive education across the world. During the conference a forceful statement relating to the education of children with SEND was passed, stating that inclusion should be the goal for all children with SEND. The statement continued to postulate that:

> mainstream schools should accommodate all children whatever their need whether that be physical, intellectual, social, emotional, linguistic and all other conditions. (CSIE, 2018: 1)

During the conference they devised a framework of action which recommends that all educational policies should state the intent that primarily children with SEND should be educated in their local mainstream schools.

The framework makes many suggestions relating to the educational provision of children with SEND, with the most significant being:

- **every child** has the right to an education and to be able to achieve an acceptable level of learning which is appropriate to their individual needs
- **every child is unique**
- education systems should be drawn up and implemented to **meet the diverse needs of children**

- those children with SEND **must have access to mainstream schools** which focus on child led pedagogy
- inclusion into mainstream schools is the **most effective** way of dealing with discriminatory attitudes and processes. (UNESCO,1994)

The framework continues to suggest to governments that:

- future policies and budgetary provisions are made for children with SEND
- inclusive practice should be adopted as a matter of law or policy
- each child should be 'given a voice' in their own education through whatever system of communication is most appropriate
- more funds should be invested in the early identification of SEND and early intervention programmes.

It is important to note here that all of these documents are statements that recommend practice and that, although the UN Convention is legally binding, it will be up to the countries concerned to implement them in their own way. There are some critics of the Convention. Edwards and Davison (2015) suggest that decisions relating to the ability of children to have capacity to comment on their rights will usually be made by adults, and they question whether children really do have the freedom of thought suggested. They go on to question whether the Convention reflects a 'westernised' (p. 71) approach to children's rights which may not be as possible or relevant to those living in the developing world where resources and training for education may be sparse.

REFLECTION

- Do you see it as important that there are national and international rulings around the education of children with SEND?
- Is there anything in the UN Convention that surprises or concerns you?
- Are your surprised by the groundbreaking work/views that the Salamanca Statement upholds, particularly as it was written in 1994?

CASE STUDY 1.1

George

George was born in 1956 to a professional couple who were both teachers. His parents had spent some time in Ethiopia working as missionaries but moved back to the United Kingdom whilst George's mother was pregnant as they wanted to

(Continued)

receive pregnancy care in the UK. George was born a couple of weeks early and his parents were delighted.

George's early development was slow. He did not sit independently until he was around 18 months and gradually health professionals diagnosed him as having moderate learning difficulties. His speech was also slow to develop, but as his mother was a teacher she was able to do lots with him to support his development. At this time in the UK's education history early years provision was not a priority.

When George was four his parents started to make plans for his education and they started talking to their local Infant school – at this time inclusion was not a priority for schools. However, after many meetings and conversations George was able to start Infant school – to begin with he attended in the mornings, increasing to full-day provision after the first term. When the time came for him to move to Junior school more conversations ensued, but because George's experience of inclusion was so positive and he was doing so well it was agreed that he would attend his local mainstream Junior school.

To begin with this went well; however, as he got older his development seemed to slow down and he was not making the same progress as his peers. It was decided when the time came for George to move to Senior school that he should go to a small local special school. Here the class sizes were smaller, there were better staffing ratios and different learning styles were catered for. George once again began to flourish.

At the end of George's time in education he moved on to college and continued to study his new-found love of baking and cooking. He managed to get a job working in a small café where adults with learning difficulties were employed to make cakes and serve in the café.

Consider

- Do you view this as a positive story of inclusion?
- Why might it have been that George made less progress in the Junior school?
- How different might this story have been if George was growing up now?

1988 EDUCATION REFORM ACT

In 1988, the Conservative government under the leadership of Margaret Thatcher launched the National Curriculum (NC). This ensured that all children across the country would receive the same educational curriculum wherever they lived. Gold et al. (1993) were concerned about the introduction, stating that the curriculum may be seen as a

> set of constraints which will inhibit teachers to such an extent that the individual needs of children with SEND will be ignored. (p. 55)

Jones (2016) reports that in the spring of 1997 the Conservative Party lost their first general election in 18 years.

The final section of this chapter will focus on history to the beginning of the 21st century. At this time New Labour came into power under the leadership of Tony Blair. The new government particularly espoused the need for 'social inclusion' which valued all citizens and sought to give them a voice in situations that involved them.

EDUCATION POLICY IN THE 21ST CENTURY
EARLY YEARS CURRICULUM - 2000

The Curriculum Guidance for the Foundation Stage was introduced in 2000. In many areas of the country, schools built nurseries that offered part-time early years provision, which ensured that when children entered school they were better able to cope with its demands and were better acclimatised to the expectations of school (Education England). The launch of this curriculum was an attempt to offer standardised provision to young children across the UK whilst accepting that it may be delivered differently depending on the kind of provision accessed. In relation to children growing up with SEND, it suggested that settings should:

- follow an inclusive ethos and all families should be welcome in the setting
- ensure that no child be excluded because of their ethnicity, faith, gender, family background or ability
- encourage early years practitioners to celebrate the life experiences of all families and children.

The document was the first to suggest areas of learning for young children and these were:

- personal, social and emotional development
- communication, language and literacy
- mathematical development
- knowledge and understanding of the world
- physical development
- creative development.

BIRTH TO THREE MATTERS - 2002

In 2005, a new curriculum was developed by Sure Start to meet and address the many expanding childcare places. Birth to Three was developed to ensure that all children were encouraged to be competent learners from birth. The curriculum recognised that as younger children were going into childcare, a better quality provision needed to be available for those whose needs were not met by the Curriculum Guidance for the Foundation Stage. The framework offered settings the opportunity to recognise the 'holistic nature of child development', whilst encouraging practitioners to plan according to each child's unique needs and fascinations.

EARLY YEARS FOUNDATION STAGE - 2008

In 2008, the government combined the Curriculum Guidance for the Foundation Stage, Birth to Three and the National Standards for Under 8s DayCare and Childminding, and developed the Early Years Foundation Stage. This new amalgamated policy was to be used for all children aged between nought and five. It introduced for the first time into settings the principle of the unique child, which suggests that:

> every child is a competent learner from birth who can be resilient, capable, confident and self assured. (DCSF, 2008: 5)

The document goes on to state that the diverse needs of children should be celebrated, and introduced the requirement that practitioners should offer 'personalised learning' that promotes 'positive attitudes' to diversity and difference (p. 6). The document introduces seven areas of learning, which are:

- communication and language
- physical development
- personal, social and emotional development
- literacy
- mathematics
- understanding the world
- expressive arts and design.

It continues to suggest that practitioners must plan for the individual needs of all, and that discrimination must be challenged. The curriculum makes the case that the best way for young children to develop and learn is through play that can be instigated and led by children themselves and facilitated by qualified practitioners. The policy, as with the previous Curriculum Guidance for the Foundation Stage (Department for Education and Employment/Qualifications and Curriculum Authority [DFEE/QCA], 2000), stressed the importance of ensuring that all children should be included whatever their needs. Since 2008 the EYFS has been reviewed, cut back and some would suggest become more bureaucratic (Roberts-Holmes, 2015; Save Childhood Movement, n.d.). Ang suggests that the purpose of early years education is an 'intensively debated topic' across the world (2014: 185) and that parents are increasingly being put under greater pressure to send their children to 'good schools' that will place 'them on the right track to a successful education' (p. 186). She likens this to 'hot housing' children before they are ready into a standards-driven education system. Roberts-Holmes holds a similar view and suggests that education across the world has become a 'global race' (2015: 303) which begins with the early years. Ang continues to critic the Early Years Foundation Stage Profile (EYFSP), which seeks to assess and record the learning of the very youngest children and which gives a formal assessment of young children's attainment at the end of the EYFS stage. Whilst it is important to ensure that children are developing and learning, profiles such as this can profligate concerns about children who may not have reached certain developmental profiles and may therefore be seen by some as having SEND. Carr (2001) argues that models of assessment that highlight 'problems or deficits' are not helpful and may cause undue worry for parents.

DEVELOPMENT MATTERS - 2012

In 2012, Early Education with support from the DFE produced a document called Development Matters. This document follows the four themes of the EYFS:

- the unique child
- positive relationships
- enabling environments
- learning and development

and introduces to practitioners the concepts known as the 'characteristics of effective learning' (COEL), which are:

- playing and exploring – engagement
- active learning – motivation
- creating and thinking critically – thinking.

This document is used widely in early years settings as it is a little more inclusive and focuses on the holistic development of young children. It will be discussed further in Chapter 5.

REFLECTION ————————————————————

- Is provision in your setting always facilitated by knowledgeable practitioners who know how to develop children's learning?

- Are children in your setting encouraged to lead their own play or are you being encouraged to promote more literacy and numeracy activities?

- Do you feel that early years provision is being compromised by a government that is more concerned by standards?

SPECIAL EDUCATIONAL NEEDS CODE OF PRACTICE - 2001

The Special Educational Needs (SEN) Code of Practice (DFES, 2001) set out for the first time the following definitions of SEN:

- children have a special educational need if they have a significantly greater difficulty in learning than the majority of children of the same age; or
- have a disability which prevents or hinders them from making use of educational facilities of a kind generally provided for children of the same age in schools within the area of the local education authority
- are under compulsory school age and fall within the definition at (a) or (b) above or would do so if special educational provision was not made for them.

As well as initiating legal requirements for families of children with SEND, the Code sets out to ensure that children were better able to access education in mainstream settings within the community in which they lived. The policy also put into legislation steps that nurseries should take if they suspect that a child in their setting has a SEND. Carpenter (2005) states that the Code addressed the importance of early intervention services which did not just contribute to children who had been born with some kind of disability or genetic condition, but also supported those children who for a variety of reasons were not developing in line with their peers. The Code also identified the need for

- partnership working with parents, ensuring from the start of concerns regarding a child that parents should be informed all the way along of what support there is for them and their child
- closer relationships with agencies from health, social care and education in the form of multi-agency working
- pupil participation – ensuring that wherever possible the voice of the child is heard.

The policy sets out the process that families had to go through to ensure that their child was eligible for a Statement of Educational Needs first introduced through the Warnock Review. These statements, which were to be written alongside parents by a practitioner known to the family, set out the particular needs of the child. They discussed any support they may need in terms of extra resources and staffing and often brought with them a pot of money from the local authority (LA) to be available to the child's setting. As with most areas of policy making there are people who questioned the inclusivity of statements. Booth suggests that any document that singles out particular learners as needing an individual education plan, setting out the 'deficits' (2000: 92) of the child and the support that child will need in order to make progress, is not inclusive. However in my experience families valued these statements as they set out the legal requirements of what their child was entitled to, and gave them a voice in the resources available to families.

Another aspect of the Code of Practice was the introduction of a Special Educational Needs Co-ordinator (SENCO) in every early years setting across the country. It was their role to work closely with families and children, ensuring that their needs were being met both at the early stages of diagnosis – early years action – and after diagnosis of a condition – early years plus (DFES, 2001).

EVERY CHILD MATTERS - 2003

This paper was launched after the horrific murder of Victoria Climbié, a child who was raised by her African family in the UK. Victoria suffered shocking systematic abuse, eventually dying. One of the main issues within the Climbié case was that the family did not speak English. After the Laming Report which was issued due to this and other murders of children by their parents, the Every Child Matters paper was launched. It sought not just to avert child deaths, but also to ensure that a child's voice was heard more readily, through safeguarding procedures. This paper was divided into five sections promoting that:

- every child should be healthy
- every child should stay safe
- every child should be able to enjoy and achieve
- every child should make a positive contribution and be able to participate and have a voice in decisions which affect them
- every family should be able to achieve economic wellbeing (HM Government, 2003).

As part of the Every Child Matters programme Sure Start centres were launched initially in the most economically deprived areas of the United Kingdom. These centres were originally drawn up in a comparable way to the Head Start programme in the USA, which was established in 1964 (Office of Head Start, 2018). Sure Start centres were developed over the coming years and were eventually found in most communities across the country. However, critics of the centres felt there was no real 'blueprint' relating to what services they should offer (DFE, 2011). This was partly because they were intended to meet the needs of individual communities and these will differ from one place to another. In 2011 an evaluation was carried out by the Coalition government on the work of Sure Start (DFE, 2011), and although some positive aspects were highlighted relating to the improvement of children's communication skills, an improvement and higher take up of immunisations, other services were found to be lacking.

In terms of support for children with SEND there were varied views as to whether these were effective. Parents particularly favoured the fact that many services were under the same roof and that early intervention was available, particularly for pre-school children. They also welcomed the opportunity for children to interact with their peers through parent and toddler groups. However, there were also negative issues. Some of these related to the centres taking a long time to decide which services they would be offering and issues with measurement of the improvements that had been made in families' lives. Unfortunately, with the changes in government since 2010, less money has been allocated to Sure Start programmes and in many areas of the country these services have been closed (Morton, 2018).

TOGETHER FROM THE START - 2003

This document was produced in 2003 in order to both establish and support the need for greater multi-agency working for those involved with children with SEND. The publication particularly supported the view that there should be:

- more active partnership with parents
- rapid and better coordinated assessment of needs
- recognition of the importance of key workers to support families and children with SEND (The National Archive, 2003).

Once again, this document supported the need for early intervention to support children at the very start of their lives and for this to continue until the children went into school. The document's discussion of the need for each family to be given a key worker was seen, at that time, as a positive step forward (Barnardo's, 2001). Before this it was often the case that a family may have had many professionals from different agencies working with the family and child. The appointment of the key worker sought to ensure that one person, who should be known, trusted and supported by the family concerned, should coordinate these services. However, Revels (2015) suggests that this may be an area of provision that practitioners do not feel equipped to take on. This may be due to their seeming lack of experience as well as the view that other agencies may want someone from a similar background to take on this role.

This document also set out a programme called Early Support, which

aimed to improve the way that services work with parents and carers of disabled children and young people from birth to adulthood across health, education and social care. (Council for Disabled Children, n.d. a)

CASE STUDY 1.2

A personal note

I had started working as a Sure Start services co-ordinator in a city in the North of the UK. Previously I had worked as a Portage worker with a local authority and as the Special Educational Needs Co-ordinator in a children's centre in the Midlands. In terms of qualifications I had a BA (Hons.) Early Childhood Studies degree and an MA in Inclusive Education, as well as many years of experience working with children with SEND. I had always struggled when other professionals asked me which service I came from, as because of the multi-agency nature of much of my work I didn't really feel that I sat in 'education' alone but equally I was not a 'health professional' either.

Early on in my time at the centre I felt it was important to make links with the local doctors' surgeries and health visitors as the centre could support and enhance their services. I was also keen to share my experience of working with children with

SEND and felt that this was something we could work together on – I felt a personal commitment to multi-agency working with families.

At the end of my first meeting with the health visitors I was preparing to leave when one of them asked me what my professional qualifications were. When I told her she became quite negative, suggesting that a person who had 'in the main worked in education could not possibly know how to work with health professionals'. I was lost for words and a little bit hurt by her comments. However it is fair to say that as the years passed we did work together well.

Consider

- Have you ever experienced negativity like this?

- If so, how did it make you feel?

- Do you feel that there are 'hierarchical' barriers to multi-agency working?

SEND CODE OF PRACTICE 0-25 YEARS - 2014

In 2014 a new SEND Code of Practice was introduced by the Department of Health and the Department for Education jointly. This document now covers children from ages 0 to 25 and relates also to children with disabilities as well as those with learning difficulties. It seeks to move away from the categorisation/labelling of children according to a syndrome/illness or disability. However Runswick-Cole and Hodge (2009) assert that the new Code should be replaced by a 'Code of Practice for Educational and Health Rights', as this would move away from the deficit/medical model of SEND that still prevails through education.

The widening of age seeks to ensure a better transition for young people with SEND. The definition of SEND remains the same, but the new Code focuses more on the active participation of children and young people in matters that affect them as well as relating to a more child-/person-/family-centred approach. The document goes on to to give guidance on the joint planning and commissioning of services for children with SEND.

The new Code introduced a new Education, Health and Care Plan (EHCP), which replaces the previous Statement of Educational Needs, giving greater advice on how to carry out statutory duties to identify, assess and improve outcomes for children with SEND.

One of the more controversial elements of the new Code of Practice is the changes made to the evolving role of the Special Educational Needs Co-ordinator (SENCO). This role is now seen as a more strategic one whereby the SENCO becomes a senior leader and has to be a qualified teacher who is prepared to undertake training at master's level. Whilst this would give the person required a better level of knowledge, Crutchley (2018) suggests that the role has become far more managerial, therefore leaving maybe younger and less experienced practitioners to undertake more of the one-to-one work that children with SEND need.

THE EQUALITY ACT 2010

The Equality Act (Gov.UK, 2010) brought together individual acts relating to sex discrimination, race relations, disability, gender and employment rights, and makes the requirement that settings should make 'reasonable adjustment' to ensure that children with SEND are educated in mainstream schools. However the Act gives no real guidance as to what the term 'reasonable adjustment' means and therefore it is left to the discretion of head teachers and managers (Borkett, 2012). In terms of practice the Act sets out that settings should:

- provide a service which children with SEND should be able to access
- work closely with local authorities in both identifying a child's needs and working with the family in ensuring that the child's needs are adequately met
- ensure that no child should be discriminated against.

The Act also sets out similar requirements for practitioners working in settings in terms of employment rights.

THE CHILDREN AND FAMILIES ACT 2014

In 2014 the Coalition government introduced this Act in order to 'make provision in relation to children, families, and people with special educational needs or disabilities' (p. 1). The Act, which particularly related to the newly written Special Educational Needs and Disability Act (DFE and DOH, 2014), sought amongst other duties to

- explain the responsibilities and functions of local authorities in supporting children with SEND
- ensure greater multi-agency working
- promote integration.

It is interesting that this Act uses the term 'integration' rather than 'inclusion'. Savage discusses the view that integration often related to people who appeared to be 'outsiders' (2015: 4) or who were excluded from society in some way. This does not seem to me to be about true inclusion, which views all to be unique and which celebrates difference and diversity.

In 2015 the Conservatives won a general election and since then many of the policies mentioned in this chapter have been removed. Added to this, local authorities have had their budgets slashed and are unable to support children with SEND in the way they had been under prior governments. Recently the Children's Society has put out the following statement:

We are deeply concerned because we know from our own specialist services and our research that these Government cuts to local services hit the most vulnerable teenagers and children hardest. (2018)

EARLY YEARS FOUNDATION STAGE - 2019

During summer 2019 changes were made to the EYFS. According to the Montessori group these will focus more on the strengthening of children's language development. Statistics indicate that more than one in five children begin primary school with speech and language difficulties (Save the Children, n.d.). The inclusion of measures to support children's language development whilst in the early years will hopefully make a difference to these figures.

There will be a drive to strengthen children's literacy and numeracy outcomes. The inclusion of these has caused some controversy by groups that feel that particularly comments around numeracy are not supported by empirical evidence and will detract from other more important elements of the curriculum (Early Education, 2019). It is hoped by the government that these changes will result in children being better prepared for Key Stage 1.

Alongside these have been changes made to the Development Matters document, which finally seems to be gathering some positive recognition from government. Early Education congratulates the government on this and their recognition of the Characteristics of Effective Teaching and Learning (COETL). The document will be simplified and made more succinct for practitioners to use; however, the content of the document will remain unchanged. It will continue to cover the seven areas of learning introduced throughout the EYFS in 2008. It has been stressed that this document should not be used too prescriptively as these areas are a guide to children's development, and that decisions made in this regard should be firmly rooted in sound evidence by practitioners who know and understand young children's development.

From reading this chapter you will have discovered the 'power' of policy and how it affects the everyday life of practitioners and children. You will also have discovered that there are many policy documents that relate to children with SEND and that all settings should be aware of. It always alarms me when I go into early years settings that many are completely unaware of the SEND Code of Practice (2014) as this is paramount if there are children in the setting with or who may become children with SEND.

Through this chapter you will have:

- understood why legislation and policy are a fundamental part of education
- been made aware of how policy relating to special needs was first introduced and how it developed both nationally and internationally during the 20th century
- considered how policy has changed during the early years of the 21st century and the implications of this to families and children with SEND.

The next chapter will focus on inclusion and the importance of this particularly in early years practice. It will discuss what it is and how it supports children in the earliest years who have or may be thought to have SEND.

END OF CHAPTER QUESTIONS

- How has this chapter supported your knowledge of the importance of legislation and policy?

- How do you feel that you have become more aware of the policies that link to the early years and working with children with SEND?

- How will you share with others information that you have gained from this chapter?

FURTHER READING

Ang, L. (2014) Preschool or prep school? Rethinking the role of early years education. *Journal of Contemporary Issues in Early Childhood* 15 (2): 41–52.

This reading from Ang discusses some of the more contentious issues that are going on in the early years at the moment – issues such as the way play is excluded from the early years in favour of phonics and 'readiness for school'.

Baldock, P., Fitzgerald, D. and Kay J. (2013) *Understanding Early Years Policy* (3rd edn). London: Sage.

This book from Baldock, Fitzgerald and Kay is a very good guide to the importance of legislation and policy and why it is necessary in early years practice.

Crutchley, R. (ed.) (2018) *Special Needs in the Early Years: Partnership and Participation.* London: Sage.

This book edited by Rebecca Crutchley is a very useful textbook which raises and discusses many issues relating to partnership and participation when working with children with SEND.

2

THE DILEMMA THAT IS INCLUSION

Having focused on legislation and policy in the previous chapter, the importance of inclusion will now be discussed.

By the end of this chapter you will:

- understand concepts of exclusion and how they link to the principle of inclusion

- be aware of the ever evolving nature of inclusion and how it has changed over the years

- consider the importance of teamwork and alterations to practice that can enable settings to become more inclusive.

As the title of this chapter suggests, inclusion is a concept that is multi-faceted and complex with people having their own views and opinions on what inclusion means to them. Others' views and opinions may well affect the way they deal with certain groups of people within society, depending on their own experiences of inclusion. However before the concept is discussed and understood, it is important to first focus on the practice of exclusion and to consider groups that are excluded from society.

The chapter will then move on to focus on principles relating to inclusion. The history of inclusion will be introduced and recognition made of how it has developed over the years. Concepts and understandings that have changed views of inclusion will be discussed within the context of the 'unique child', a term that has been fostered through each edition of the Early Years Foundation Stage (EYFS) document first introduced by the Department for Children, Schools and Families (DCSF) in 2008.

The final section of this chapter will consider how settings can become more inclusive, and will discuss practices that can be adopted firstly to evaluate and then to reflect on the inclusiveness of the setting. Throughout the chapter, questions will be asked of the reader, encouraging you to reflect and ponder on your own views and experiences. Case studies will also either introduce dilemmas in practice or give ideas of how practice can be changed to ensure greater inclusion.

WHAT IS MEANT BY EXCLUSION?

Volf (1996) suggests that the modern term of inclusion cannot begin to be understood without first critiquing exclusion and how this manifests itself in practice, going on to state that exclusion occurs in all areas of society, through educational institutions, science, media and belief systems. He makes the point that before the term inclusion is fully understood one needs to consider which groups are excluded from society or, as he prefers to say, are excluded from 'the norm' (p. 58).

Douglas (1966) believes that people exclude because they are uncomfortable with anything that blurs the edges of their everyday lives or disturbs their own identities and 'cultural maps' (p. 78). These views suggest that sometimes it might be ignorance that causes people to exclude – not because they intend to, but because they are unaware of practices that may fail to acknowledge certain groups of people. This suggests that more education is needed for practitioners in order that they can be better equipped to work with families and practitioners who are different from them and who may have different views, particularly relating to special educational needs and disability (SEND).

In education terms, exclusion can mean many things. It can be considered when a child has misbehaved in school and has been punished by being removed for a defined period of time. The Coram Children's Legal Centre (CCLC) reports that in 2016 children with SEND accounted for 7 out of every 10 children excluded from schools. Since then the Department for Education (2018d) has produced statistics that indicate that the number of school exclusions rose from 6685 in 2015–2016 to 7720 in 2016–2017. In primary schools the numbers of exclusions rose during this time by 0.03%. Children with SEND who have a Statement of Educational Needs or an Education, Health and Care Plan are six times more likely to be excluded than other children. The CCLC (2016) continues to draw parallels between school exclusion and young people who end up in the criminal justice system, many of who may have some form of SEND. This would suggest that exclusion in school-aged children can lead in later years to crime. Interestingly, the CCLC points out that exclusion must not occur as a consequence of the child's needs not being met in a school. However, if a child's needs are not met, this may then result in bad behaviour which may go on to cause an exclusion. As well as this, Harris (2018), writing for *The Guardian* newspaper, states that many children with SEND have not yet been given a school place and therefore are being denied an education. Added to this he suggests that local authorities (LAs) are experiencing high levels of financial cutbacks which are having an impact particularly on children with SEND due to teaching assistant numbers being cut and resources in schools being squeezed. In 2012 the then Children's Commissioner Dr Maggie Atkinson recommended that no primary school should ever exclude a child in Reception or Key Stage 1. However, in 2008 Garner suggested that more than 4000 children under the age of five were being excluded from the school system.

Recently there has been much concern that the current government's plans to roll out more grammar schools across the UK will only add to more divisions in education as another way of excluding children because they may not meet the required criteria for entry into particular schools. Harris goes on to suggest that the government's willingness to open more grammar and free schools will also have an impact on children with SEND. In 2018 Borkett discussed the difficulties of the current 'standards driven education system' in the UK, suggesting that this may have an impact on children with SEND. Slee and Allan (2005: 17) and Henninger and Gupta (2014: 36) endorse this view, suggesting that the 'pernicious regimes of inspection' also have an impact on the number of children with SEND that schools might take: Currently schools advertise their statistics through league tables which parents may peruse when making their choice of school. If a school accepts a significant number of children with SEND then this may have an effect on their league table statistics which could prevent parents from viewing it as a good school.

These figures may appear lower than other schools in a community. This in itself can mean that schools become wary of taking in children with SEND. Recently the term off-rolling has been discussed by educationalists. The term relates to

> the practice of removing a pupil from the school roll without a formal, permanent exclusion or by encouraging a parent to remove their child from the school roll. (YouGov, 2019)

This may be done before an Ofsted visit to schools and so goes along with the view that children with SEND can affect the academic achievements advertised through league tables.

Exclusion can also relate to the practice of children with SEND being educated in a mainstream school but spending much of their time away from the rest of the children in small groups with children similar to themselves. In this situation one might ask the question why the children are in mainstream schools when they spend the majority of their time away from their peers. Here begins a debate that has been ongoing since Mary Warnock suggested in 1978 that children with disabilities should be, wherever possible, educated in mainstream schools (Education in England, 2012). This decision began the dilemma of inclusion that has continued for many years. Currently in the United Kingdom it is not unusual to find mainstream schools that have a separate unit for children with some kind of special need. These are often called 'enhanced resource facilities'. In these provisions children will spend some of their time being taught in the unit and spend other time taught in mainstream classes. Hunt (2018) states that these models can be contentious and asks whether this is real inclusion, suggesting that these units might create an 'us and them' thinking for staff working in them.

PERSONAL NOTE 2.1

I was working in a mainstream senior school with a child who had some level of physical disability. This meant that she struggled to get from classroom to classroom on time and had difficulties accessing some of the equipment used, in the main during science-related subjects. My role was very much based around the pupil's health and safety. It was announced that the class would be going on a trip to one of the science-based activities nearby as a recent attraction was based around the chemistry that the class recently had been studying. However, when the letters to parents went out there was not a letter for this child's parents. When I challenged the teacher about this she replied that because of this child's physical needs she could not be included on the trip. I went home and reflected on the response.

The next day I returned to the teacher and sensitively told them that this action was discriminating against the pupil involved. I suggested that I could accompany them on the trip – in my own time – thus ensuring that they benefited from it as all the other children would. The teacher spoke with the head teacher and it was agreed that this should happen.

Sometimes when focusing on the needs of children with SEND practitioners have to have a voice in the provision for those children.

REFLECTION

- Focus on a time in your own life when you have been excluded as the pupil in the case study was. How did it make you feel?

- Consider which groups of people are currently excluded in society? How many can you name?

- How might you help to support those who may be excluded or have been excluded in the past?

SOCIAL EXCLUSION

Social exclusion is a term that has become widely used by sociologists, academics and educationalists in the past 50 years. Levitas (1998) suggests that the term is ambiguous and is a complex, multidimensional process that is dependent on many factors. It can relate to the taking away of specified services and resources to particular groups of people. This can then have an impact on certain groups who may have no way to communicate their needs and rights. For those affected, it may have a negative impact on the way they are able to live their lives. Levitas et al. (2007) suggest that social inclusion can affect children and families in different ways and can result in 'severe negative consequences for quality of life, well-being and future life chances' (p. 9). Many of the examples of social exclusion relate to the way particular groups of people are ostracised or looked down upon by others within society. The situation alluded to previously, relating to grammar schools, could be considered as one of these.

Another example of social exclusion is where families do not feel that they can participate in services that are available to them. Collins (2003) suggests that the factors in the non-participation of families are often individual and may well relate to the family itself. It may be about the environment or the building where groups are run, the dominant language used in the group, family circumstances and how well a family has been welcomed. The following case study discusses a situation that took place in a Sure Start centre in the Midlands with a family who were new to the United Kingdom.

CASE STUDY 2.1

Jose

Jose moved from Slovakia with his family to the UK in 2009. He was the youngest, at nine months, of two children and was born just before his parents left their home country in search of a 'better life'. His brother was six and started school immediately they moved to the UK. His parents moved with just a few belongings and were given a flat to live in. Many other families from Slovakia were housed in the same area and the local Sure Start group supported the families with groups, equipment and childcare where they could come together and talk about their experiences. Jose's mother had just started a course in childcare whilst living in Slovakia and she was keen to continue this in the UK.

As time went on it was noted that Jose's skills were not developing quite as quickly as they should have been. The health visitor kept an eye on this and

(Continued)

when he was around 18 months old made a recommendation that the Portage team within the centre should start to visit Jose and his family. Thus began a pattern of fortnightly visits where the worker would take toys into the home, encouraging Jose to engage with them and to learn new skills. However, there was a language barrier – whilst Jose's mother knew some English it was not enough to support these sessions. One of the things that Portage requires is for parents to log, through a diary, the child's success with the tasks. The Portage team got together and devised some new paperwork which, rather than relating to words, used symbols and sticky stars to congratulate the child. These new sheets were further developed by the centre and used with many other families over the course of five years.

Sometimes when engaging with families, time-honoured ways of working need some adaptation. Just a small adjustment to the paperwork ensured that Jose's family was better supported and were able to access a service which they could have been excluded from before.

Consider

- Are there families who access your setting who need adaptations to services in order that they are included?

- Where are the barriers in early years settings that prevent them from supporting certain groups of society?

REFLECTION

- In what ways does your practice support families?
- Could you do more to support families?
- How could settings better support families of children with special needs?

In 2006 Kay et al. suggested that

social inclusion is about being enabled to take part – having any barriers to involvement lowered if not totally removed – and having the right to participate. (p.344)

Nutbrown and Clough agree, stating that social inclusion is 'framed within policy documents, which problematises the social exclusion of particular groups' and excludes them from society (2009: 198).

Having focused on exclusion, the chapter now moves on to discuss the concept of inclusion, seeking to determine what it is and how it affects children and their families.

WHAT IS INCLUSION AND HOW HAS IT EVOLVED OVER THE YEARS?

As a starting point to this section of the chapter I asked a group of students studying for a Foundation Degree in Early Years to come up with some of their own views of what inclusion is – these are their responses:

> Inclusion is respecting everyone's individuality by recognising and celebrating their differences and culture and providing everyone with the opportunity to express their voice. Inclusion is unique to every individual.

> Inclusion can be defined as celebrating and including the unique individual, promoting good wellbeing and diversity.

> [T]he recognition that every child is unique and is entitled to their fundamental rights and choices. It enables all to develop a deep sense of belonging supporting them to be valued.

REFLECTION

- Having read the students' responses try and write your own definition of what inclusion is.

- How easy was it?

Inclusion is a multifaceted principle that has evolved over the years. In Chapter 1 you were introduced to the work of Mary Warnock, who in 1978 was charged by the then Conservative government to carry out an evaluation of the education of children with SEND (Parliament UK, n.d. a). At the end of this Warnock recommended that children with SEND should, if possible, be educated in their local community schools rather than being sent to institutions away from their homes. Another recommendation was that families and professionals from health, education and social services should work together more collaboratively and produce a Statement of Educational Needs for each child (DFES, 2001) – this has now been superseded by an Education, Health and Care Plan with the introduction of the new Special Educational Needs and Disability (SEND) Code of Practice (DFE and DOH, 2014). Both documents set out the nature of the child's needs and how they should be met by the various professionals working with the family and child. These documents are important because they also enable money to be set aside to support children through their education. It is, however, interesting to note that Warnock changed her views on inclusion in 2005. She stated that rather than being a positive thing, the move to ensure that all children with SEND should go to their local community school had been a 'disastrous legacy'. Warnock felt that since her first report so many schools were opening doors to children with SEND that it was having a detrimental effect on normally functioning children in schools.

Corbett (2001) views inclusion as being a 'freeing' concept that relates to the empowerment of people and the need to encourage all and celebrate diversity and difference. This suggests that the more children grow up to recognise that they are all different, the more they will develop this understanding as they continue to grow into adulthood. Savage (2015) takes Corbett's views one step further by suggesting that inclusion should be part of 'a healthy instinct in a strong confident society' (p. 5).

CASE STUDY 2.2

Joseph

Joseph is seven years old and has Down syndrome. He is a very happy, strong-willed little boy who enjoys singing, dancing, being outside and being with his friends. He has an older sister who he loves and talks about quite often. Joseph struggles with his communication but uses Makaton well. He has been supported since birth by the local authority Portage team. When Joseph turned four his parents had to make the decision regarding which school to send him to. He had attended a nursery with an enhanced resource unit but his parents were keen that he should go to the same school his sister went to in the community.

The school was anxious about this but agreed to him starting his first year in reception with a full-time teaching assistant (TA). The year went reasonably well, but Joseph became frustrated at times because he couldn't make his needs known. This meant that he often had temper tantrums and could be aggressive to other children. Because of this Joseph was often taught alone in a small room with his TA and only joined the other children at playtime. The school became more concerned that Joseph's needs could not be met in this particular school. Still his parents fought for this mainstream place but would become angry if, at the end of the day, Joseph's diary said that he had been playing with the water (which he loved) as they did not view this as 'real learning'. They did not seem to appreciate that, due to his cognitive skills, he could not do the work that other children in the class could do.

It was decided that Joseph needed some input from teachers who were trained to teach children with special needs, used Makaton as a main form of communication and could better tailor Joseph's education to his needs. It was decided that he should spend half the day in a special school and would then be transported back to the mainstream school in the afternoons. However, Joseph became very confused by this and his behaviour deteriorated. He could not cope with the different expectations in both schools and he became more and more frustrated in the mainstream school. Lots of things were put in place to support Joseph. A diary for both settings was set up, a visual timetable was put in place, but he became more and more angry and would not go in the taxi back to the mainstream school. This resulted in him hurting both his TA and the taxi driver. After the second year it was decided that the mainstream school was not right for him and so he moved to the special school on a full-time basis.

Consider

- How could the mainstream school have supported Joseph more effectively?

- How could Joseph's parents have been better supported by the mainstream school?

- What would you have done to support Joseph through his split placements?

WHAT IS THE DIFFERENCE BETWEEN INTEGRATION AND INCLUSION?

In the past, the term 'integration' was used more when considering the education of those who were seen as 'different' from the norm (Borkett, 2018). Savage discusses the view that integration was often related to people/children who were thought of as being 'outsiders' (2015: 4) or who were excluded from society in some way, so this may include children with SEND. Rix (2011), when identifying integration, suggests that practitioners often acknowledge the 'normally developing children' whilst failing to acknowledge all children who attend the school and who may appear different from others. According to Corbett (2001), integration was more concerned with adaptations to existing practice and the notion that a child had to 'fit in' with the practice of the setting, rather than the setting doing all it could to enable the child to attend the school and to put in place all the extra resources to ensure that the child could be welcomed and belong to the setting.

Rix goes on to suggest that maybe practitioners consider groups of people who seem to be different according to their own stereotypes. This is sometimes known as the 'deficit' model, which views certain groups of people as being less important than others. Children may be disadvantaged for many reasons, but for the purpose of this book, I will be discussing particularly the needs of children who have SEND. The 'deficit' model goes along with the 'medical model' of disability. The medical model suggests that disability is something that can be treated or cured with the use of medicine. It is thought of as being a negative term which focuses on the 'problem' that the child may have and the medical services that they need in order to ensure that they can lead as full a life as possible (University of Leicester, 2015). In the 1980s, groups of people with disabilities believed that this model was outdated and too negative, and so the 'social model of disability' was introduced. This model suggests that rather than disability being about the disabled person, it is society that disables children. This may be through services that are offered or through access to buildings, etc. (University of Leicester, 2015).

WHAT CAN PRACTITIONERS DO TO TRY AND CHANGE PRACTICE IN RELATION TO DIVERSITY?

So how do practitioners seek to understand inclusion and view difference as something positive and exciting? The Centre for Studies on Inclusive Education

(2004) produced the Index for Inclusion in 2002 . This document encourages settings to look beyond categories of inclusion and to ensure that practice is appropriate for all children and practitioners. It encourages a whole team approach to consider issues of diversity which should include people who may feel that they are on the periphery of a team, such as midday supervisors, caretakers, office staff and students on placement. The Index encourages all to discuss the ethos, mission and practice of the setting to ensure that it is fully inclusive. Throughout the Index, there are both discussion and suggestions of how settings can change practice in order to become more inclusive. It extols the need to rewrite outdated policies with a whole team approach, and to recognise, as Nutbrown and Clough (2009) do, that inclusion is a matter of social justice.

Corbett (2001) and Baldock (2010) suggest, however, that at times practitioners who are involved in such projects may just be paying 'lip service' (2010: 70) to diversity and inclusion without fully understanding or wanting to understand the importance of inclusion – this can mean that the support becomes 'tokenistic' rather than it being planned and meaningful. Corbett challenges practitioners to think about the individual needs of every child and to ensure that settings become a 'listening community' (2001: 95). At times this can be difficult for practitioners as they may have deeply held beliefs that need to be challenged, or the way they behave to particular groups of children might need addressing. It may be that old ways of working need to be reconsidered, new resources acquired, activities adjusted, but this is all part of what becoming an inclusive setting is about (Purdue, 2009).

INCLUSION RELATING TO SEND

The concept of 'inclusion' particularly related to children with SEND is seen as being a positive notion, but Barton suggests that it is also a 'euphemism for the failure of education to meet the needs of all children' (1987: 48). Slee and Allan endorse this by suggesting that it encouraged 'hierarchies of those who are included in regular life and those who live in the margins and beyond' (2005: 15). Both of these comments may suggest that the term is about groups of people with SEND who find themselves on the edge of everyday life. More recently, Brodie and Savage (2015) have suggested that the previous two comments may still be apparent when considering the needs of young children, and that inclusion can still be seen as the consideration of those who might be outsiders and are therefore excluded from certain groups. Ainscow (2000) says that inclusion is a continuous battle against processes and procedures within society and education which may alienate particular groups of children. However if one looks at the Salamanca Statement (UNESCO, 1994), which was highlighted in Chapter 1, we see that this refers to the following groups of children:

all children regardless of their physical, intellectual, social, emotional, linguistic or other conditions. This should include disabled and gifted children, street and working children, children from remote or nomadic populations, children from linguistic, ethnic or cultural minorities and children from other disadvantaged or marginalized groups. (p. 6)

Surely this indicates that inclusion relates to all children. In 2013 Waitoller and Artiles viewed inclusion as being 'a global movement that emerged as a response to the exclusion of students who were viewed as different' (p. 330); however, it is important to recognise that other countries and cultures do not view inclusion in the same way as it is perceived in the UK. This may be due to limited funds, a lack of training around inclusion, or the belief in some communities that disability relates to witchcraft or the work 'of the devil' (Borkett, 2018: 81). Whilst these views may seem somewhat strange to those of us living in the developed world, it is important to recognise that the United Kingdom is a multicultural nation where people from many different countries come to live and work. Cultural beliefs can prevail even when people have lived in the UK for many years.

Nutbrown and Clough (2009) also view inclusion as a human right, discussing its importance to a child's identity whilst stating that if a child is not included or valued then this may lead to the child feeling isolated, which may go on to affect their self-esteem and emotional wellbeing. Moss (2007) views inclusion as a democratic right for all children, and challenges every practitioner to rethink their policies and practices to ensure that the rights of all children are met.

In Chapter 1 we saw how, with the introduction of the Early Years Foundation Stage (EYFS) document by the Department for Children, Schools and Families (DCSF) in 2008, the then Labour government charged early years practitioners with viewing all children as being unique, thus avoiding any of the previous categorisations of children. It is interesting to note that the concept of the unique child has prevailed despite the fact that this document was written over a decade ago and there have been many changes made to the policy over the years due to changes in government. Hunt (2018) suggests that the uniqueness of children is easier to recognise in the early years as the Early Years Foundation stage offers a child-centred approach to learning which is based around close observation of children's interests, fascinations, communication and the ways that they prefer to learn.

The view that inclusion relates to all children is shared by Nutbrown and Clough (2009), who view the principle as being about citizenship. They argue that the more children experience difference and diversity in a positive way, the more they will grow up to value and celebrate all human life.

Swain and Cook (2005) view inclusion as more of a philosophy or a way of being that values and celebrates difference. They advocate that not only does it refer to people but it also relates to the breaking down of barriers such as buildings, policies, support systems and communication methods. They go on to suggest that inclusion should challenge practitioners to make fundamental changes in practice to ensure inclusion for all. This supports the view that practitioners should continually reflect on their practice in order to make changes that will have a positive impact on all children. Nutbrown et al. (2013) view inclusion as exciting, whilst stating that it is vital for all children to value diversity and difference. Whilst many would share this view, it is important that the principle is recognised as being challenging and can depend not only on principles and practice but also on practitioners' deep seated views.

REFLECTION

- Why is it essential to talk through ideas and views relating to inclusion with other students or people you may work with?

- Look again at your definition of inclusion. Has it changed since reading this section of the book? If so, why?

- Are there children you know who might be excluded from activities they would like to be involved in? Why might this be, and could you do something more to include these children?

Brodie and Savage (2015) support the view that inclusion should be an ever changing and evolving concept which will constantly develop depending on the needs of families and children involved in the setting. They discuss the view that inclusion is not just a human right but is also about belonging. However, they too offer a word of warning to practitioners that they may need to consider their own views and prejudices about inclusion and what this means to them, before a team can come together and truly offer an inclusive service. This can be taxing and therefore needs careful leadership to build a truly inclusive setting.

The final section of this chapter will discuss the importance of teamwork and alterations to practice that can enable settings to become more inclusive.

It is important to acknowledge, as the Index for Inclusion does, that inclusion is concerned with the collaborative participation of practitioners as well as children and families (CSIE, 2002). As mentioned earlier, inclusion sometimes needs practitioners to question and reflect on their own views of the concept (Borkett, 2018). This can be a challenge as discussions like this have to be sensitively led by someone who understands and acknowledges that people's deep-seated views and personal experiences can sometimes shape or impact on how they work with particular groups of children and families.

Teamwork is vital in all aspects of childcare but especially when working with children with SEND. Teams can also incorporate other agencies and so it is vital that all concerned are transparent and working cohesively to support the child and family. The Index for Inclusion is a very good resource which can encourage a team of people to really focus on making the setting more inclusive.

A WHOLE TEAM APPROACH TO SUPPORT INCLUSION

It is not, and should never be, one person's responsibility alone to ensure that settings are inclusive. Although the updated Code of Practice suggests that primarily it is the strategic role of the Special Educational Needs Co-ordinator (SENCO) (DFE and DOH, 2014), if a setting is going to be fully inclusive, it needs every member of the team to be on board. This begins with the ethos of the setting and its fundamental aims that should relate to all families and children (Brodie and Savage, 2015). An inclusive ethos should:

- reflect the values the setting seeks to promote
- respect all children and parents – trying to support them or having the knowledge to be able to signpost them to different services
- encourage and inspire all children
- support children to ensure they feel secure and that they belong
- develop inclusive policies and procedures as a 'whole team approach'
- ensure that everyone's voice is heard, including those of parents and children
- creative an environment which reduces 'barriers to learning' (Centre for Studies on Inclusive Education [CSIE], 2004: 4)
- promote positive relationships between adults and children (Pugh, 2001: 1).

PERSONAL NOTE 2.1

Our own experiences can affect our views of inclusion. As a young child I had a great friend who had SEND and was educated in a mainstream school up until the age of 11. This was in the early 1960s, so a while before Warnock had started her work. I learnt a lot from watching the struggles that her parents went through in order to ensure that she had an education that responded to her needs and enabled her to develop.

I also have a nephew with severe learning difficulties, and I have watched the battles that his parents have been through to get him into a mainstream school and to receive support throughout his life. It has taken up a lot of time and affected them emotionally. I think both of these situations have had a major impact on how I view inclusion in terms of both the child and the family. At times these experiences can be positive, but at others not so.

As a governor of a special primary school I hear regularly how the school has half-termly school council meetings where children are asked about things relating to the school and what is being done there. Through different communication systems

(Continued)

such as Makaton and technology the children are able to give their views on matters that affect them.

Consider

- Is this something that your setting does? If so, how effective is it? If not, is it something that you could start?
- How much does your setting 'really listen' to the voice of the child?
- Would you need to consider different communication systems to ensure that all children's voices are heard?

REDUCING BARRIERS TO INCLUSION

Once the team has worked together on creating the ethos, it is then important to consider any barriers that need to be addressed. These may relate to the building, resources in the setting such as toys, books, the outdoor area or communication methods. Sometimes an audit might be needed in order to evaluate how effective the setting is. Children can be involved in this through discussions, time sample observations (Rose and Rogers, 2012) and photographic information collected in the setting. Picture books of things that the setting has done or has been involved with are a really powerful way of encouraging children to discuss and evaluate the environment, resources and activities.

COMMUNICATION SYSTEMS

As was discussed in Chapter 1, the UN Convention on the Rights of the Child (UNICEF, 1989) sets out that all children should have a voice in matters that involve them, so it is vital that children are given a voice in some way. However, often children with SEND may struggle to communicate orally so may need different communication systems to ensure their voice is heard. It is important here to consider that currently in the United Kingdom there are 1.4 million children who have long-term speech and language difficulties. In areas of deprivation around 50% of children go into school with communication difficulties ('I CAN', 2018). Therefore it would appear that communication is not just an issue with children who have SEND. As part of inclusive practice it is important that settings are made 'communication ready'. So how might that happen? There are many strategies that can be used to ensure that children recognise and respond to different types of communication. The following are suggestions of different forms of communication which may support children with SEND.

MAKATON

Makaton is a very effective tool which uses signs and symbols to communicate (Makaton, 2017). It is very important to acknowledge here that signs and words should be used together; this helps children to understand that there is a link between signs and the spoken word. The Makaton symbols can also be used as labels for boxes of resources, and with students alongside text offering them a pictorial symbol that helps them to understand what the text says. However, some parents of children with SEND can be concerned that if their children are using signs then they may not develop their talking. Sheehy and Duffy (2009) carried out research with schools that regularly used Makaton, discovering that as years have gone by Makaton has become more widely known and more popular and an effective tool for children developing their language. Added to this, a popular children's TV programme regularly uses Makaton and so its popularity in the mainstream has increased (British Broadcasting Corporation [BBC], n.d.).

OBJECTS OF REFERENCE

Another resource that is very useful and a particular tool for children who may have no communication is that of objects of reference. These are resources that can be used because of their 'sensory properties' to make a link to an activity (Communication Matters, 2018). They were originally developed to support children who were visually impaired but are now used widely in education. They were used regularly with a child who only seemed to communicate when he was angry by banging his head on the floor. He was introduced to a basket that included the following:

- a key – sensory room
- a hairbrush – if he wanted to relax (he loved having his hair brushed)
- a plastic cup – snack time
- a plastic knife and fork – dinner time
- a picture of a tap – to indicate he could play with water
- a fifty-pence piece – he was having his daily walk to the shop
- a photograph of his house – home time
- a purse – for the trip to the shop.

Jones et al. (2002) found that objects of reference were also effective when used alongside Makaton for children with severe and profound learning difficulties.

CASE STUDY 2.3

George

George was five years old and attended a special school. He had severe learning difficulties and struggled to understand basic commands. His physical skills were well developed and he was able to walk and run. However, he had no verbal understanding

(Continued)

and often became very frustrated when he could not make his needs known. When George became frustrated he would often bang his head on the floor or on any other furniture that were nearby. It was important that George was offered a system of communication that he could understand and that gave him a voice and the ability to make a choice of simple things such as food or drink. It was decided by the staff team that objects of reference should be offered to George to see whether this supported his communication. His parents were consulted and they agreed that this would be a good move for George.

Because of George's needs he had an adult with him all of the time. That person changed throughout the day so that George did not get used to one adult solely. George also had quite a strict routine to his day, which involved time in the sensory room and usually a walk to the local shops. He really enjoyed both of these activities and so it was decided that these should be the activities first used for the objects of reference. In a basket we placed a purse (for the trip to the shop) and a key for the sensory room. Each time George was offered these activities the object was offered to him. Gradually he started to make links between the activities and the objects. So we added more objects, which included a nappy when he was changed and a photograph of his home for home time. George's tantrums seemed to diminish and gradually more objects were included in his basket.

Consider

- How important is it for you that all children should have a voice in matters that affect them?

- What different systems of communication might you use in practice?

- How might you move a child on from objects of reference?

REFLECTION

- Do you know of children who struggle to communicate or who use different communication systems?

- How effective are they and what challenges do they bring?

- Do you see them as inclusive for all children?

AN INCLUSIVE ENVIRONMENT

It is also important when trying to offer an inclusive setting that the environment is appropriate for children and their families. This means that it should include pictures, writing and symbols that represent the children and families attending the setting. For children with SEND whose physical skills are not yet fully developed, it is important that they have adequate space to move around in but also space where they can sit and be still. This is also important for children who are on the autistic spectrum and who may become overstimulated. Wooden toys and resources are vital for children with SEND as some of the more colourful toys are not as appropriate for children. The toys that are more appropriate for children with SEND will be discussed further in Chapter 5, which relates to play.

Through this chapter you have:

- understood concepts of exclusion and how they link to the principle of inclusion
- become aware of the ever changing term 'inclusion' and how it has evolved over the years
- considered how inclusion can and should become a principle adopted in all early years settings.

The next chapter will focus on the purpose of early intervention, and how this has evolved over the years and led to what we know it as in the present day. We will also focus on programmes of early intervention in a critical and analytical way.

END OF CHAPTER QUESTIONS

- How has this chapter supported your understanding of how exclusion can prevent certain groups of children from being included?

- Inclusion has improved drastically over the past 50 years, but what are some of the challenges of inclusion in the 21st century?

- What do you see as your role in ensuring that inclusive practice is maintained?

FURTHER READING

Borkett, P.A. (2019) Inclusion and participation. In: Fitzgerald, D. and Maconochie, E. (eds) *Early Childhood Studies*. London: Sage.

This chapter discusses the importance of inclusion and introduces the reader to the concept of the unique child (EYFS). It goes on to discuss the importance of participation for all children to have a voice through whatever mode of communication they prefer.

Centre for Studies on Inclusive Education (CSIE) (2004) *Index for Inclusion – Developing Learning, Participation and Play in Early Years and Childcare*. Bristol: CSIE.

(Continued)

This handbook is a very comprehensive tool that can support teams in ensuring that their practice is inclusive to all children. It looks at inclusion in its widest sense and recommends a whole team approach.

Jones, F., Pring, T. and Grove, N. (2002) Developing communication in adults with profound and multiple learning difficulties using objects of reference. *International Journal of Language Communication Disorders* 37 (2): 173–84.

This article focuses on the importance of supporting children with moderate and profound learning difficulties to communicate in whichever way they prefer.

3

EARLY INTERVENTION

Having focused on the importance of inclusion in the previous chapter, this chapter will examine early intervention and its importance in the lives of children and their families.

By the end of this chapter you will:

- understand the origins of early intervention and how it has evolved over time
- consider some of the programmes that relate to early intervention particularly with children who have or maybe are thought to have special educational needs and disabilities (SEND)
- examine some of the benefits and challenges of early intervention.

This chapter will begin with an attempt to identify what early intervention is and to focus on some of the historical reasons as to why these programmes have been established. The chapter will consider the organic nature of intervention and how it has changed over time. The ecological systems theory initiated by Urie Bronfenbrenner will be introduced as this theory establishes how children and families can be supported on different levels by various agencies.

The chapter will then discuss some of the programmes currently used in the UK with young children with SEND, which include Portage, Picture Exchange Communication Systems and the Sonrise programme.

The last section of the chapter will focus on some of the benefits of early intervention programmes, considering how they support children and families. However, it is also important to address some of the challenges that can emerge with children, and particularly their families, when following such programmes.

Within this chapter the views of a number of early years practitioners currently working in settings or who have links with early intervention have been sought. Whilst I had previously worked in this field, I wanted to gain up-to-date views of how services are currently offered as well as the benefits and challenges of them.

WHAT IS EARLY INTERVENTION?

As has been discovered in previous chapters, many concepts in early years practice have different meanings depending on who would be reading the book. The Early Intervention Foundation describes early intervention as the ability to:

> identify and provide early support to children and young people who are at risk of poor outcomes such as poor academic attainment and mental health problems. (2018: 5)

According to the House of Commons Library, it is:

> a public approach which encourages preventative intervention in the lives of children or their parents to prevent problems developing later in life. (2017: 3)

A number of charities support the view that to offer prevention to families in the early years is more cost effective than offering it later on in life when issues such as truancy, crime and mental health may emerge (e.g. Barnardo's, 2011; Health Foundation, 2018). Graham Allen, a member of the Labour Party, was commissioned by the Conservative Prime Minister David Cameron to carry out a review in 2011 to evaluate how early intervention was being used across the United Kingdom. Allen viewed early intervention as being a principle that offers the country an opportunity to make lasting improvements in the lives of children and their families, going on to concur with the House of Commons that early intervention can make 'long term savings' (2011: 5) in public spending. A similar review was carried out by the then Labour MP Frank Field, which particularly focused on poverty and the opportunity to change families' life chances through intervention and other programmes.

In 2008 John Bercow, later Speaker of the House of Commons, led an advisory group which sought to review services for children and young people (aged 0–19) who had communication needs. This paper suggested that early intervention refers to the prompt involvement of professionals who support the child and family. It also, as with other papers, points out that money spent on multi-agency support early in a child's life can help children who may be at risk of poor outcomes to do better and achieve more through education. Ten years later the report was reviewed by I CAN (2018), a charity that supports children with speech and language difficulties. This stated that in the UK 1.4 million children struggle with their speech and language, suggesting that if these issues can be prevented early on in children's formative years through programmes of support, it could avert these problems escalating and causing emotional issues later on in life. The review also discovered that there was a lack of speech and language therapists to support children, and that staff in settings do not always feel well-enough trained to support early intervention programmes for children who need them.

Alternatively, the House of Commons Science and Technology Committee in 2018 referred to early intervention as being the opportunity to 'take action to resolve "problems" as soon as possible before they become more difficult to reverse' (p. 3).

Though in these definitions there are no real links to SEND, there is an understanding that early intervention relates to the opportunity to support children and their families to improve their life chances, thus hoping that children will go on to become adults who can hold down a job and ultimately bring money into the economy.

It is important to realise here that there is a strong link between poverty and SEND. The Joseph Rowntree Foundation (2016) suggests that poverty is both a cause and an effect of SEND. It states that children with SEND are more likely to be born into families on low incomes and who are living in poverty. These children are more likely to develop SEND throughout their lives, particularly in relation to speech and language and poor literacy skills, and are therefore more likely to need interventions in school.

EARLY INTERVENTION AND SPECIAL EDUCATIONAL NEEDS AND DISABILITY

Blann (2005) describes early intervention as being the support offered to children and their families from birth to age three who have particular developmental challenges. The European Commission in 2013 supported a similar view suggesting that early intervention strategies should support the development of children with SEND and their families. The SEND Code of Practice (2014) suggests that for children from 0 to 5 who have or who may be thought to have SEND, these programmes should be giving training to parents in using early learning programmes which promote and develop play, language development and communication skills. They recommend that this should be done initially in the home, and should also include support for families who might be coming to terms with a diagnosis of SEND for the first time.

In 2012 the Coalition government under the leadership of David Cameron sought a review of early intervention services that particularly supported children with SEND (DfE, 2012). Interestingly much of this review focuses on speech and language, and whilst we know that this is important for children with SEND, it is not always the only issue that they may have. The review discovered that intervention programmes do support children's development, but – similarly to the Bercow review – that practitioners need more training and support in learning how best they can support young children's development.

We can see from this section that early intervention can take many forms and is something that Coles et al. (2015) view as being problematic. They comment that their research found that it can be disparate and mean different things to different people.

I wondered what the practitioners I consulted with felt about the importance and value of early intervention services.

- A speech and language therapist viewed it as 'responding to a need as it is identified using an evidence base to inform good practice'.
- An early years practitioner who has been a childminder, worked in Children's Centre and is a Special Educational Needs Co-ordinator (SENCO) views it as 'the support that practitioners can give to children and their families at an early stage'.
- An early intervention worker for a local charity sees early intervention as 'directly involving children and their parents supporting children to overcome the challenges they experience because of their SEND'.

So again here we see contrasting views as to what early intervention relates to.

REFLECTION

- What is your understanding of the term early intervention?
- Does it relate to particular groups of children?
- Have you had any experience of early intervention?

HOW HAS EARLY INTERVENTION CHANGED OVER THE YEARS?

Hannon and Fox (2005) explain that early intervention is not a new concept and suggest that the establishment of the health visitor role, this first began a service of early intervention in the 1900s, was to support families living in cramped conditions with poor sanitation and high levels of infant mortality. Adams (2012) reports that the first course for health visitors was established in 1916 and that the role always focuses on the promotion of public health and prevention of ill health. Since 1916 the numbers of children being born has increased caseloads but health visitors still work with vulnerable groups either by supporting these individuals themselves or by signposting them to other services.

In 1918 the Education Act offered funding for nursery education, thereby introducing the concept that if children have access to good-quality nursery education at the ages of three to five they will go on to do better in formal education (Parliament UK, n.d. b). In 1972 a framework was set out to expand nursery education and in 1996 nursery vouchers were introduced to all four-year-olds. In 1997, four-year-olds were offered free nursery education. This has now been expanded to younger children if there is a particular need for them to be in early education. Although we might view this as education it is also preventative, as it ensures that children who are struggling in any way with their development can be identified earlier and the right kind of intervention provided.

Hunt (2018) suggests that Warnock was one of the first to postulate the effectiveness of early intervention in 1978 when she suggested that the education of children with SEND should begin as early as possible. She skilfully acknowledges the role that parents and practitioners can play when early intervention is introduced.

In 1999 the Labour government set up its 'flagship' programme Sure Start, which was discussed at length in the previous chapter (DfE, 2018c). This enabled early intervention to be available for families and children in one central building and with many agencies working collaboratively. Sadly, as governments have changed and local authorities' budgets have diminished, this service is being phased out in many areas.

In 2003 the Early Support programme emerged as a tool for children with more complex needs. This was a groundbreaking programme which sought to recognise the uniqueness of children as suggested in the Early Years Foundation Stage (DCSF, 2008). The programme acknowledged that children with SEND often have a plethora of other professionals working with them, and ascertained that these professionals needed more of an integrated approach to their work. The Early Support programme suggested that an initial report should be put together at the start of working with a family: this detailed the child's disabilities and the circumstances around them, thus negating the need for the family to retell their story over and over again. These professionals may come from education, health, social care or charitable organisations. Another requirement of the pro-gramme was regular 'team around the child' meetings, which discussed the continuing needs of the family and child. These would be chaired by the family's key worker, who might often be the Portage worker or someone working in a setting that the child attended. However this proved controversial as practitioners from other agencies wanted their practitioners to be the key workers. Recently a parent I spoke to whose six-year-old daughter has been diagnosed as being on the autistic spectrum told me that she had repeatedly had to tell practitioners about her daughter's difficulties over and over again. She stressed that each service would ask her why it was that she was concerned. This made her feel powerless in the life of her child.

Much of the work that has been demonstrated in the previous paragraph is referred to as multi-agency work. This means that there may be a team of prac-titioners from education, health, social care and local charities working alongside the family and child. The Early Support programme sought to ensure that these agencies worked closely together in order to support the child and their family. Through changes in governments these teams have continued but under differ-ent names – the term 'team around the family' is now referred to. This recognises that it is not just the child but the family that needs ongoing support.

Both SEND Codes of Practice (DFES, 2001; DFE and DOH, 2014) clearly set out the requirements of early intervention to be home based, thus supporting the very youngest children who have SEND. When the first Code was intro-duced this was a new initiative; as policy has evolved, this has become a very important aspect in supporting the youngest children with SEND.

In 2012 the National Health Service (NHS) developed a health check to be carried out with parents after consultation with any setting that the child may attend. This is to ensure that development is on track and that there are no development issues with the child. If there are concerns, the child might be referred to the local authority for further assessment.

In 2017 the government offered free childcare for two-year-olds. This was to be offered initially to vulnerable children who for one reason or another needed early support through quality childcare. One of those vulnerable groups is chil-dren who have SEND. Through research carried out by Georgesen et al. in 2014 it was discovered that in order for children to develop well through early years education they:

- require a quality setting
- necessitate a well-qualified workforce with practitioners who understand the importance of child development and how to support children appropri-ately in their very early years
- and that staff receive relevant training, particularly when working with chil-dren with SEND.

However, one might ask how you define a quality setting (Borkett, 2018). There are many differing views on what constitutes quality. The research also discov-ered that often it is the youngest, least qualified practitioners working in baby rooms which results in many staff not feeling adequately trained to work with babies and toddlers or children with special needs.

So how do some of the practitioners asked see the evolvement of early intervention?

- An early intervention worker stated that it constantly evolves and is dependent on new research that informs policy makers in order to make changes in the lives of children and families.
- An early years practitioner makes similar comments whilst suggesting that as early intervention proves its worth, it will become more and more important in the lives of children. This is a view shared by a speech and language therapist (SALT); however, she feels that sometimes early intervention services are 'being designed to meet the provider for instance the local authority or the National Health Service' rather than meeting the needs of the children who require it.
- A Portage worker suggests that early intervention has changed rapidly over the years, but with this comes an increase in the number of children requiring it. As discussed earlier, she believes that there needs to be better training of practitioners to particularly meet the needs of children with SEND.

CASE STUDY 3.1

Jamie

Jamie was two years old and living in a disadvantaged area that had a Sure Start children's centre within it. When his mother went to the clinic for his two-year check up she said that she was concerned about Jamie's speech and language. He had a repertoire of around 15 words, which was a little under what you would expect of a child at that age. Jamie was referred to the Portage team in the centre and to the speech and language therapist (SALT). To begin with, the SALT and Portage worker went out to observe Jamie. He had lots of toys but his Mum said that he did not particularly like books – a tool that all Portage workers use to encourage literacy with young children. After the visit it was decided that Jamie would receive fortnightly support from the Portage worker and be seen by the SALT in three months.

Visits were made and he particularly enjoyed bubbles, balls and cars but, as his Mum said, he had little interest in books. Gradually Jamie's speech improved and he began to say more words, and when the SALT visited after three months she could see a big improvement in his language.

But what about the books, you may well ask? The Portage worker decided to make a book about Jamie, his home, his parents and the things he liked to do. She included lots of photographs of important people as well as some of his favourite toys. Gradually he became more interested in the book and took it everywhere with him. Over a period of time picture books were introduced to him and slowly his interest in books increased. Jamie was a real success. Early intervention for six months was enough for him to feel confident in using language and gradually he saw

(Continued)

the importance of books. Here is a wonderful example of how integrated services can come together and make a difference to the lives of children.

Consider

- What in particular do you think helped Jamie's development to improve?

- In what way do we see the positive influence on Jamie's life?

- In what ways will this support prepare him for his education?

PERSONAL NOTE 3.1

I have worked in early intervention for much of my working life, starting in 2001 around the time that the first SEN Code of Practice was launched. During that time early intervention was, in the main, based around SEND. However, as time has moved on and research has been carried out that extols the difference it can make to young children and their families, early intervention has a much wider remit now and relates to a wider group of children, particularly those living in the most disadvantaged areas of the country. I see this as very important, but I am slightly concerned that it means that rather than focusing on the causes of children's needs, we may become a little too fervent to label these children as having special needs when maybe they, just like Jamie, simply need some support in a particular area of their development.

THE ECOLOGICAL SYSTEMS THEORY

When focusing on early intervention it is important to consider this theory as it views all aspects of a child's life as organic and evolving. It also recognises the place of other professionals and agencies that may be linked with the child. The theory was instigated by Urie Bronfenbrenner, a psychologist born in 1917. Gray and Macblain (2015) postulate that Bronfenbrenner's work suggests that children constantly change and that life experiences and what is going on around the family through policy, society and history can have an effect on the development of children and their families. Bronfenbrenner recognised that children who grow up in deprived areas have a tendency to make less progress in education than their counterparts living in more affluent areas.

Bronfenbrenner views development occurring 'within a multitude of different but nested contexts' (Gray and Macblain, 2015: 50) that he believes have a direct impact on a child's learning and development. He views the environment as being one of those areas, suggesting that children learn through the environment and the people around them. His theory takes the form of four concentric circles placed within each other (Figure 3.1). Gray and Macblain (2015) suggest that a similar way to view this theory is that of a set of Russian dolls with the smallest being at the centre.

MICROSYSTEM

The child is believed by Bronfenbrenner to be central to the theory. Inside the first circle sit the parents, siblings and peers who the child has regular contact with. It includes the community and neighbourhood where the family lives, and practitioners who work with the child and family. This might include early intervention workers if the child has SEND. In earlier illustrations of this theory, the faith system that the child may grow up in is significant. Whilst this is not such a focus in children's lives these days, it is important to note that families coming to the UK from abroad with children with SEND can hold very strong faiths and may have some slightly different views of disability than those held in the UK (Borkett, 2018).

MESOSYSTEM

The next part of the systems theory relates to areas of life that the child is directly involved in, so this might be the home, the community in which they live and the setting. The theory suggests that these elements are not static but that the microsystem and mesosystem relate to one another. So the relationships that the family has with all of these elements are constantly evolving and changing. This can be observed particularly when a child starts school and new relationships are built within the school. Suddenly parents may feel that they have less say over their child's upbringing. Children make new friends and are required to conform to new ways of being that are asserted by teachers rather than their parents. The parents of children with SEND can feel particularly vulnerable at this time, when they have spent so long caring for their child.

EXOSYSTEM

The next layer of the theory relates to school governors, local government, the parents' workplaces, mass media and local industry, and again relates to relationships that this layer has with the others. An example of this might be, as was mentioned earlier in the chapter, the government's policy to extend free childcare funding to children under the age of two who are living in disadvantaged areas. This layer would also relate to the part that the local authority (LA) may take concerning how policies are implemented in settings. Initially the government sets policies, but then it is up to the LA to cascade them into settings.

MACROSYSTEM

The final layer of the theory focuses on cultures, faith, legal and societal institutions, as well as dominant beliefs and ideologies that pervade society. So if we take the example of the free funding, the dominant belief with this is that quality childcare will support disadvantaged families and hopefully have a positive impact on their future education.

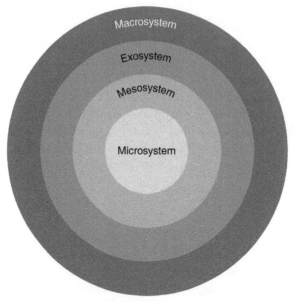

The individual child at the centre

Microsystem – family, practitioners and peers
Mesosystem – school, community, faith setting, media
EXosystem – parents' work, child's school
Macrosystem – nationally held views and beliefs, policies, customs and laws

Figure 3.1 Bronfenbrenner's ecological systems theory

There have been many diagrams illustrating this theory over the years, in the form of Russian dolls and concentric circles with some including arrows to demonstrate the relationships between each system. However, by being circles with unbroken lines I am not sure that this correctly displays the relationships that flow between the layers, a view concurred by Rogoff (2003). Instead of the concentric circles I would rather view Bronfenbrenner's theory as ripples within a pool (Figure 3.2). When a pebble is thrown into a pool it creates ripples, which move in relationship with one another; they quickly evolve from one circle to two, three and maybe four ripples. For me this better illustrates Bronfenbrenner's ecological systems theory (Borkett, 2018).

Figure 3.2 Bronfenbrenner's theory represented through ripples

- How does Bronfenbrenner's theory support you in understanding that development does not just relate to the child but to the family and other areas of society too?

- Which professionals may support the early intervention of young children?

- Have you had any experience of being with a child who has been supported with early intervention, and what do you see as the benefits of it?

EARLY INTERVENTION PROGRAMMES

This section of the chapter will focus on some of the early intervention programmes used here in the UK. There is not enough capacity in this chapter to discuss them all at length, therefore it is probably best for you to research those that interest you and the websites specified will give you more information.

Before we focus on the programmes available it is important to consider when early intervention might begin. The SEN Code of Practice (DFES, 2001) states that a child is thought to have a special educational need if:

- they have a significantly greater difficulty in learning than the majority of children of the same age; or
- have a disability which prevents or hinders them from making use of educational facilities of a kind generally provided for children of the same age in schools within the area of the local education authority
- are under compulsory school age and fall within the definition at (a) or (b) above or would so do if special educational provision was not made for them.

Therefore some children with a SEND will start early intervention almost straight after birth. These might be children for whom something had been picked up through an ultrasound scan before birth or children who may have a sensory impairment such as hearing or sight difficulties that is discovered immediately they are born. Children with Down syndrome, spina bifida and some medical impairments may receive early intervention from the start of life. If a child is not developing alongside their peers or there appears to be some kind of developmental delay, parents will need to first seek advice from their health visitor or doctor. If they too have concerns, the child may be recommended to the local authority for extra help through early intervention. Also practitioners in early years settings may be concerned that the child is not reaching their developmental milestones. This could mean that professionals may work with parents and children in the child's home to support their development.

It is important to note here that not all children who have difficulties with their development will be identified at this early stage. Unfortunately it is not uncommon for children with speech and language difficulties or who may, later on in life, get a diagnosis of autism, attention deficit hyperactivity disorder (ADHD), dyspraxia or dyscalculia, or children with social and emotional problems, to enter nursery before any kind of support is offered. This may be for a variety of reasons:

- the family may not have picked up any difficulties with the child
- the family may not want to recognise that the child is struggling in an area of their development
- some of these difficulties do not show up in a child until they are older.

This means that not all children receive early intervention and so have to wait a little longer for badly needed support. As practitioners, therefore, it is important that parents are listened to and supported if they have concerns about their child's development.

Table 3.1 describes some of the early intervention programmes used in the UK.

Table 3.1   Early intervention programmes currently used in the UK

Name of programme	Origins of programme	Theoretical underpinning	What it seeks to do
Portage	Wisconsin, USA. Came to the UK in 1976	Based loosely around Vygotsky's zone of proximal development and Bruner's scaffolding.	Portage is a home-based early intervention programme. Portage workers delivering the programme go into the child's home and work with their parents to deliver a play-based programme in order to develop a child's holistic development. This support continues until the child goes into nursery provision, whereby the Portage worker will support practitioners during a transition phase. For further information see – www.portage.org.uk/about/what-portage
Picture Exchange Communication System (PECS)	Originated in America in 1985	Based loosely around Skinner's view on operant conditioning. This relates to the suggestion that if an action is reinforced positively the child will continue to use the action.	PECS focuses on communication and has many stages. Trained professionals known as 'communicative partners' work with a child, encouraging them to communicate through the use of pictures. This 'partner' will encourage the child to give the partner a card in exchange for something such as a chosen activity or an item of food or drink. As the child becomes more and more proficient the child builds up a repertoire of symbols to communicate. Speech is encouraged alongside the pictures to enable the child to see that the two are linked. For further information see – www.pecs-unitedkingdom.com/pecs

Name of programme	Origins of programme	Theoretical underpinning	What it seeks to do
Makaton signs and symbols	Established in the UK by Margaret Walker, a speech and language therapist, with Kathy Johnston and Tony Comforth in 1978	Based around the view of Jerome Bruner that children sometimes need a support system of knowledgeable adults to encourage children's communication.	Makaton is a sign and symbols programme that is used *alongside language* with children who have some kind of developmental or speech and communication delay. Professionals can be trained to use Makaton and is especially effective if used in the early years. It has become quite well known partly due to the focus and use in CBeebies TV. For further information see – www.makaton.org
British Sign Language (BSL)	Originated around the 18th century, particularly in communities where deaf people lived		A language system that incorporates sign, visual language, facial expressions, gesture and body language. For further information see – www.ndcs.org.uk/information-and-support/language-and-communication/sign-language
The Son-Rise Program	Originated in the USA in 1970 by two parents who were looking for a way of communicating with their children who were autistic	Based loosely around Vygotsky's zone of proximal development and Bruner's scaffolding.	The programme is centred around the child and views them as being unique, wonderful and amazing. It goes on to create a style of interactions where the adult takes their lead from the child rather than the other way round. For further information see – www.autismtreatmentcenter.org/uk-next-steps
Early talk boost	Run by I CAN, the charity that supports children's communication skills	Based on Bruner's views that children require an adult or a peer to support the building of language skills.	This is an intervention carried out by specially trained practitioners in settings. It gives targeted intervention of 15–20 minutes three times per week, and seeks to give children skills in speech, language and communication that will enhance the learning of new words, support children with speech and language difficulties and track children's progress. The programme supports parents too as they are required to reinforce the skills that their children are taught through the sessions. For more details please contact earlytalk@ican.org.uk

It is important to point out that this is not an exhaustive list of programmes – there are many more that effectively support children's early development.

REFLECTION

- Have you heard of any of these programmes?
- In what ways do you think they would beneficial to children and families?
- What are some of the challenges that you think might prevent these programmes from being effective?

The final section of this chapter will focus on the benefits and challenges of early intervention to both the child and their family and the practitioners working in the field of early education.

WHAT ARE THE BENEFITS OF EARLY INTERVENTION?

When focusing on this part of the chapter I chose to split the benefits and challenges into three areas. However, as would be expected, there is some overlap where one area rolls into another.

SUPPORT FOR CHILDREN

The Early Intervention Foundation (2018) makes the case that programmes can support the building of children's development, thereby affecting their social and emotional development and enabling them to learn skills that will further support them through life. Greene et al. (2015) carried out research to evaluate how the government's funding for vulnerable two-year-olds was working. They discovered that not only was it popular with children, who enjoyed attending, but it supported parents who felt that their children required more stimulation than they could provide at home. Parents reported that their children had improved speech and communication skills and that being with other children had a positive impact on their emotional wellbeing and behaviour. For children with SEND it provided them with extra support from skilled practitioners who were experienced in working with children with SEND.

Many of the programmes listed particularly relate to children's communication skills whether this is through strategies such as British Sign Language (BSL) or through Makaton. Some of the benefits of these to young children is that they give the child a voice or agency in their own lives. It can also take a lot of the frustration away from a child who wants to communicate but does not yet have the language skills to articulate their needs (Mistry and Barnes, 2013).

SUPPORT FOR PARENTS

Parents receiving support for children with SEND in the home also responded favourably regarding the programmes. Nunkoosing and Phillips (1999) report that they like to be involved with early intervention programmes such as Portage as they support families at a time in their lives when they may have received news of their child's diagnosis and need a knowledgeable adult to support them. They continue to state that the ongoing support through home visits and visits to other professionals gives tremendous help to parents when they may be feeling very vulnerable and alone.

They go on to state that they also like being involved with the setting of targets and planning of play-based activities carried out during visits, and that this gives them confidence in their ability to support their child's learning and development, as well as a 'sense of control over their child's strengths and abilities' (Rix et al., 2008: 70). However, there is some criticism of these home-based programmes. Rix et al. (2008) suggest that at times there may be a 'tension between play and therapy' whereby some parents can feel that they are, at times, more of a therapist than a parent. Bridle and Mann, both parents of children with SEND and on the receiving end of a home-based programme, felt that sometimes there was such a push on the activities that, it felt that, these activities took over and they felt bad if they took their children out to the park or shops (Bridle and Mann, 2000).

Milton (2014), a father who is on the autistic spectrum himself and has two children who are autistic, makes the case that some professionals who encourage parents to take up home-based programmes often have limited experience of autism. He argues that many of the programmes available are drawn up by professionals who have no idea what it might feel like to be disabled themselves. He questions whether such programmes can cause anxiety and stress both to children and the adults supporting them.

An early years practitioner stresses the fact that early intervention programmes should not be carried out unless parents are prepared to be fully involved. She suggests that parents who may have 'chaotic lifestyles' may not be able to commit themselves to such programmes. For these she suggests that support be tailored around the family so that it really meets their needs.

Rix et al. praise Portage for the fact that central to the programme is the family, not just the child concerned but also taking into account siblings and the extended family if appropriate. They stress the need for parents

> to have a sense of control over their family life and to recognise that effective intervention strategies result from their own actions, strengths and capabilities. (2008: 66)

SUPPORT FOR PRACTITIONERS

In relation to the two-year funding for vulnerable children there were, as always, negative aspects of this support. Staff training was an issue as not all staff felt comfortable to work with younger children. Also, when working with children with SEND, practitioners required better training to enable them to feel confident in their work with these children.

An early years manager who has been in this role for the last 20 years stated that local authority funding can be a hurdle as the criteria for funding are always changing. She points out that childcare in private and voluntary settings does not always get the same level of funding as state schools or in nurseries attached to schools.

Portage practitioners stated that at times there can be the need for them to take on skills they do not always feel well enough trained in, such as:

- counselling
- advocacy
- emotional support
- friendship.

I had experience of this once at a time when a family I was working with felt very vulnerable and isolated.

CASE STUDY 3.2

The diagnosis – Andrew

I was working with a family whose child had been referred to the children's centre as his communication skills were not developing. Andrew struggled to give eye contact, did not understand play, nor did he attempt to engage with other children. However, when working with him at home he could sustain activities he was interested in for around five minutes and he enjoyed activities based around communication, such as bubbles and books. I worked with Andrew for around nine months and he became a little more social, but there were still concerns around his development. Eventually he was referred to the local children's hospital where professionals observed his play, behaviour and communications skills.

One day I was visiting the hospital with another family and I met Andrew's parents – they explained that they had an appointment with Andrew's paediatrician, who was going to give them a diagnosis of Andrew's difficulties. I was visiting Andrew later that afternoon.

During the afternoon I received a message from Andrew's mother to say that Andrew had received a diagnosis of autism and that they were feeling distraught. I knew that Andrew's grandparents lived on the same street and so I suggested that when I visited later on in the day, Andrew went to his grandparents so that I could talk to his parents and try to explain what would happen as a result of this diagnosis. It was possibly one of the hardest visits I ever made, and yet it was good to talk to Andrew's parents and to suggest strategies that they could use to support him now he had a diagnosis. Andrew's parents felt it was important for him to be with other children, so he started attending the pre-school that we ran for children with SEND and this prepared him for being with other children.

A year later when Andrew started his transition into nursery he was better equipped to be alongside other children, to play with them and to use his vastly improving communication skills. However, what I was not expecting was the void the parents experienced when I withdrew my support. Portage is designed in such a way that after the initial transition into settings the support is withdrawn. Having been supported with fortnightly visits and going through many ups and downs, they felt distraught that this support was over.

Consider

- How important was that support for Andrew and his family?

- Have you ever worked alongside a child and family when a SEND has been diagnosed, and if so, how did it make you feel?

- Does it seem unfair to you that services should be withdrawn when the child enters early education?

As a result of reading this chapter you will have:

- understood the origins of early intervention and how it has evolved over time
- considered some of the programmes that relate to early intervention, particularly with children who have special educational needs and disabilities (SEND)
- examined some of the benefits and challenges of early intervention.

The next chapter will focus on the purpose of assessment and how this supports children who may have or have been diagnosed as having SEND.

END OF CHAPTER QUESTIONS

- What do you see as being some of the benefits and challenges of early intervention?

- How do early support programmes mentioned in this chapter support children and their parents?

- How might they also support practitioners working with children with SEND?

FURTHER READING

Bridle, L. and Mann, G. (2000) *Mixed feelings: A parental perspective on early intervention.* Paper presented at the National Conference of Early Childhood Intervention, Brisbane, Australia.

(Continued)

Although this paper is quite old, it does help you to understand how vulnerable parents can feel when they are receiving early intervention for their child. It also helps you to see how early intervention can blur the lines between being a parent and being an educator.

Coles, E., Cheyne, H. and Daniel, B. (2015). Early years interventions to improve child health and wellbeing: What works for whom and in what circumstances? *Systematic Reviews* 6 (4): 79. www.ncbi.nlm.nih.gov/pubmed/26047950

This article focuses on how issues such as societal inequalities and difficulties in health and wellbeing can have an impact on the development of children in the early years.

Early Intervention Foundation (2018) *Realising the Potential of Early Intervention.* London: Early Intervention Foundation.

This report discusses how early intervention can support the development of young children, which can have a lasting effect on their educational chances.

4

ASSESSMENT AND OBSERVATION FOR CHILDREN WITH SPECIAL EDUCATIONAL NEEDS AND DISABILITY

Having focused in the previous chapter on the importance of early intervention, this chapter will concentrate on the importance of assessment and how this can provide support to children.

By the end of this chapter you will:

- understand the importance of assessment and how it makes links to the curriculum

- see the importance of assessment in policy with particular emphasis on the Early Years Foundation Stage (EYFS) and the Special Educational Needs and Disability Code of Practice (SEND COP)

- consider the tools practitioners use to assess children and discuss the importance of the 'voice of the child' in assessment.

During the early years, children are observed and assessed on numerous occasions. This may be to determine whether children need early intervention, to discover their interests and fascinations, and to ascertain whether or not they are reaching their developmental milestones. The term assessment may be used by any number of professionals from across the spectrum of support. It is therefore pertinent to consider assessment and how this can support children and families. However, the slightly 'controversial nature' of assessment also needs to be addressed as it is often seen as a 'political hot potato' that different parties use particularly around the time of a general election (Moss, 2006). Assessment also has close links to curricula so the chapter will go on to discuss those links and how the two are interrelated.

The second part will focus on what the EYFS and the SEND Code of Practice say about assessment, particularly in relation to children with SEND. It will introduce the two levels of SEND support and describe the purpose of Education, Health and Care Plans (EHCP) and how these support the assessment of children.

The final section will discuss tools that practitioners may use to observe children and note the progress that the child is making, and will also discuss the importance of the child's voice through assessment, going on to suggest different ways in which children can be enabled to have a voice in their lives.

WHAT IS ASSESSMENT?

As with many other concepts that have been discussed in this book, the term assessment can mean different things to different people. Contact for Families with Disabled Children (2019) suggests that the term assessment is the process that social care agencies use to decide whether extra help is needed for the family of a child who may have SEND or is going through the diagnosis process. These types of assessments are called early help assessments and are often used as the starting point for families and children receiving support from a number of professionals. Basford and Bath (2014) and Moss (2006) suggest that the term from an early years perspective can become a way for governments to 'exercise control over practitioners' and that they can spend so much time assessing what children can do that they forget that part of their role is to get alongside children whilst supporting their development. Nutbrown et al. (2013: 26) assert that assessment is hard to define and make the point that there is 'confusion over much of the terminology' associated with the word. Wright et al. (1998) discuss assessment from a health perspective as being used to determine the health needs of a person and what other services they may need to support them. So we can see from these definitions that they all relate to something that is carried out by a number of services to find out what the needs of an individual are and how they can be best supported, and what other professionals may be required to work with a child and family.

Nutbrown et al. (2013) make the suggestion that there are different types of assessment. Two of which are as follows:

- Assessment for learning – this might relate to the way that a child is assessed through monitoring their development and learning against an assessment document such as the EYFS profile which is used with most children in the early years. Many documents may be used to ensure that practitioners are noting children's progress regularly.
- Assessment for management and accountability – this I would suggest is the way that settings have to proactively state how they manage their setting and are held accountable for the development of the children in their care. This can be carried out by practitioners through careful moderation of children within the school and other schools within the community.

WHAT IS MEANT BY THE TERM MODERATION?

Schools assess and monitor the learning and development of children through careful moderation. According to the National Foundation for Educational Research (2007), moderation is a term used to describe how schools create dialogue between practitioners and other professionals in order to agree on and make judgements about children's development and learning. This can be done informally through staff discussions and meetings, and through discussion with local authorities where practitioners are required to discuss and provide evidence of why they believe that children are learning at a particular level. The documentation can be in the form of observations, children's work and profiles that are being kept for the child. Then schools within a community can come together to ensure that children within their geographical area are developing at a similar rate. However, research carried out by a coalition of organisations related to early education discovered that time taken out to gather appropriate evidence of learning to complete these moderations takes practitioners away from the setting and causes extra stress and work for already pressured practitioners (Early Education, 2019). The revised EYFS agrees, stating that there is currently too much paperwork for practitioners in relation to moderation, and stresses the need for them to be able to evidence the learning of children in their care through their knowledge gained through working with children.

The Council for the Curriculum, Examinations & Assessment (CCEA, n.d.) suggests that assessment should be seen as a

systematic collection, interpretation and use of information about learning. It gives practitioners a better awareness of what pupils know and understand, what their learning experiences enable them to do and what their skills and personal capabilities are.

This quote is very positive and very much relates to what a child can do rather than what the child struggles to do, which is what practitioners should focus on.

It also discusses the personality of the child, what particular fascinations they may have and the way that they prefer to learn. The CCEA goes on to suggest that there are four types of assessment:

- Formative assessment – this relates to the formal and informal procedures practitioners take to discover how well children are developing and learning. In early years practice these often take the form of narrative observations, photographs, snapshot observations, video recording.
- Summative assessment – this may happen at the end of a term and takes the form of a document that logs the child's development and learning over a period of time, for example the Early Years Foundation Stage profile.
- Diagnostic assessment – this is the kind of assessment that is done in order to gather information about the needs of a child and how they can best be supported. The Education, Health and Care Plan, which will be mentioned in more depth later in the chapter, is an example of this.
- Evaluative assessment – this is concerned with the performance of children in a school, so it may relate to Ofsted assessments or may be how schools are represented on league tables, which parents often examine before choosing a school for their child.

REFLECTION

- Throughout our lives we all go through some kind of assessment – how have these shaped your life?
- Do you see the role of assessment as controversial?
- Do you think that children in the early years are aware that they are being assessed regularly?

THE ROLE OF OFSTED IN ASSESSMENT

During the course of 2019, the Office for Standards in Education, Children's Services and Skills (Ofsted) have been making changes to the way that they carry out inspections, which I suggest are a form of assessment of the way that a school functions and teaches children in their care. They have recently launched their equality, diversity and inclusion statement. This new document sets out the need for inspectors to assess how settings eliminate discrimination and ensure that practitioners commit to making sure that all children receive equal opportunities. This is not to say that children are all supported in the same way, but that they are supported in a way that meets their needs. The statement continues to assert that good relations between children are encouraged and fostered and that the development and learning of young children is monitored, Ofsted believe that the old inspection framework had too much of a focus on performance measures and preparation for assessments, which was to the detriment of some children, particularly those with SEND. The new framework will focus on the quality of education offered for all learners and on the behaviour and attitudes of children and how they treat one another.

This focus on behaviour is in itself something that is particularly difficult for children with SEND. The Royal College of Speech and Language Therapists (RCSLT) (2019) discuss how difficulties in speech and language can have a huge impact on the behaviour of children with SEND. They stress that if a child is not given the opportunity to communicate in some way, whether through their voice, signing, pictures or technology, their behaviour can become challenging. It will be important therefore that Ofsted acknowledge this when they are carrying out inspections and monitor the extent to which children are given the opportunity to have a voice.

Ofsted add that they will also focus on the personal development of children within settings, with particular focus on developing respectful citizens and ensuring that children recognise and appreciate diversity. They stress the importance of leaders and managers who have a clear vision for inclusion. Whilst this is vital, there is a need for that vision to be shared and welcomed by all practitioners. In Chapter 2 the suggestion was made that ensuring true inclusion requires there to be sensitively led conversations and reflections between managers and their team and that the team's ethos promotes equality of opportunity for all and a true understanding of what inclusion really means.

It would be impossible for me to fully discuss the contents of this statement from Ofsted, but more information in relation to this may be found online. The details are included in the suggested reading for this chapter.

REFLECTION

Many practitioners feel that the current inspection process produces too much work and is bureaucratic.

- How do you feel about the inspection process?
- How could it be improved?
- Are inspectors as interested in the inclusion of children with SEND – what is your experience?

ASSESSMENT AND THE CURRICULUM

When the role of assessment is discussed it is often linked to curricula. In England this would relate to the EYFS for children aged from nought to five years and then for older children the transferral to the National Curriculum. When the National Curriculum was launched in 1988 it was hailed as being quite a revolution in education terms. One of its purposes was that all children should follow the same curriculum wherever they lived and wherever they went to school. This included special schools.

CASE STUDY 4.1 ───────────────────────────

Sunflower special school for children with severe learning difficulties

Sunflower school was a special school for children with severe learning difficulties from the ages of three to eighteen. It consisted of an enhanced resource nursery for local children which also included very young children with SEND, as well as an infant, a primary and two senior classes and a further education unit. The school opened in 1978 and quickly become a popular school in the area. For the first 10 years the school had its own curriculum, which followed a mixture of practical learning and life skills. Parents chose to send their children to the school because they could understand the importance of teaching children life skills alongside more formal learning, much of which was offered through age-appropriate play activities.

However with the introduction of the National Curriculum (NC), which all schools were expected to follow, the teaching of life skills diminished. The children were expected to attain skills set out in the new curriculum. Teachers were required to adapt their teaching and to spend more time assessing children's skills.

The staff team, whilst appreciating that the NC ensured that all children received a more inclusive curriculum, found that trying to include more formal learning posed a problem. Many of the children's lower cognitive skills meant that they would struggle to learn to read or write (although that would be encouraged if possible). Many parents wanted their children to be taught life skills such as how to make a drink, feed themselves, behave with other people, go out into society, understand how to behave when going into a café or restaurant or buying something from a shop. The staff team seemed to have to be more accountable for the learning of the children than had previously been required.

Consider

- Why is it important that all children should follow a particular curriculum?

- Do you agree that a curriculum for children with SEND should be more about life skills?

- What is your experience of delivering a curriculum that may not be appropriate for all children?

In 1998 the then government brought in P levels, which were to be used with children from age five to sixteen who were struggling to meet the outcomes of the National Curriculum. These were used across the curriculum and were graded from 1, the lowest level, to 8, the highest. These levels were to be used as a tool for summative assessment and to support practitioners in making 'best fit judgements' about the learning and development of children (European Agency for Special Needs and Inclusive Education, 1998).

In 2016 a review was carried out led by Diane Rochford alongside civil servants, practitioners, parents and carers on the education of children with SEND. Some of the results of this review were that age-related assessments are not appropriate for children with SEND. The P levels were not effective and would be replaced with 'pre-key skills'. These pre-key stage standards were designed to complement wider statutory national assessment arrangements and pre-key skills would be used at both Key Stage 1 and 2 (Standards and Testing Agency, 2018).

It was agreed that schools should assess children with SEND around the four areas of need stated in the Special Educational Needs and Disability Code of Practice (DFE and DOH, 2014), which are communication and interaction, cognition and learning, social, mental and emotional health, and sensory and/or physical needs. The committee extolled the use of inclusive assessments that included the views of a range of different professionals and it was required that these should continue wherever possible for those children with SEND, particularly those in mainstream education provision. Changes were made to the ways that children with SEND should be assessed through seven particular aspects of cognition and learning:

1. responsiveness
2. curiosity
3. discovery
4. anticipation
5. persistence
6. initiation
7. investigation (Council for the Curriculum, Examinations & Assessment, 2016: 7)

PERSONAL NOTE 4.1

During the 1990s I worked in the nursery of a school for children with severe learning needs. At the time we used the early learning goals to assess the children in our care, but many of the children did not meet the criteria for these goals. As a school, alongside the local authority's support we were able to devise our own curriculum, which focused more on children's responsiveness to activities. These aligned particularly well with both the seven areas of cognition and learning and the characteristics of effective learning. It is interesting to see that over the years eminent people in SEND have become keen to assess the needs of children differently and more in line with the way that they learn.

ASSESSMENT AND ITS LINKS TO POLICY

The next part of this chapter will focus on the importance of assessment in policy documents, particularly focusing on the Early Years Foundation Stage (EYFS) and the Special Educational Needs and Disability Code of Practice.

In Chapter 1 both of the above policies were introduced. The next section of the chapter will focus more on the role of assessment and how it is described through each of the documents. Both discuss assessment in great depth, which is to be expected of guidance documents that set out the support children in their earliest years should receive if they have or are thought to have a SEND.

The documents outline the assessments children go through in their early years to monitor their development and to put in appropriate support if needed. These assessments start at birth, when babies' hearing is tested and also a heel prick test is performed which is taken in order to assess for various medical conditions (NHS, 2018). At the age of two, as was noted in Chapter 3, another assessment is carried out by a health professional alongside the child's parents, and a representative from any early years setting the child may attend. Parents are provided with a written progress check which sets out their child's development, particularly focusing on the areas of communication and interaction, cognition and learning, social, emotional and mental health, and sensory and/or physical needs (Independent Provider of Special Education Advice [IPSEA], n.d.).

If it is determined by either the parents or an early years practitioner that a child is not yet meeting the required levels of development, they will, with the parents' permission, refer the child to the local authority. They should then start to receive one of two levels of support: either special educational needs (SEN) support or they may start the process of applying for an Education, Health and Care Plan (EHCP) (Long and Roberts, 2019).

WHAT IS MEANT BY SEND SUPPORT?

This may be support given through early intervention to a child who is demonstrating some level of delay in one or many aspects of their development. It tends to be a lower level of support and can be the time when evidence is being gathered by a range of practitioners and professionals and parents, which may lead to an Education, Health Care Plan in the future. During this time, extra support can be given to the child and this support will be monitored to ascertain the effectiveness of it.

WHAT IS AN EDUCATION, HEALTH AND CARE PLAN?

An EHCP is a

> plan which identifies educational, health and social needs and sets out the additional support to meet those needs. (Gov.UK, n.d. a)

These documents set down the legal rights of the child to be supported by a range of professionals, and can be orchestrated by parents and practitioners such as a doctor, health visitor, speech and language therapist or physiotherapist. The document is drawn up by practitioners who have been working with a child who has difficulties in one or more aspects of their development. These replace 'statements' which were introduced as a result of the initial Code of Practice introduced in 2001 (DFES, 2001). These documents are for children and young people from birth to 25 and are determined by the local authority (LA) as part of their 'local offer'. A local offer relates to the support that an LA should give to 'children and young people with special educational needs or disabilities and their families' (Council for Disabled Children, n.d. b). The offer contains information about what support local authorities think will be available in their local area. These EHCPs will set out the areas of development that the child is struggling with and the required support that children should be given in order for them to develop. The plan should include

- a description of the child's SEND
- the aspirations of the child or, if this is not possible, the aspirations the parents have for their child
- what provision is required for the child – this may be in terms of which setting they should attend, what support should be offered through health practitioners and any social care support required by the family
- particular ways in which the child is able to make their needs known.

It is clearly stated through these plans that agencies should work together to provide multi-agency support to the child and their family. They should also include where possible the 'voice of the child' as to what support they feel they need. At the time of the creation of the new Code, this was seen as a positive step as the old Code had paid little attention to the importance of listening to the child.

It is important to note here that during times of austerity local authorities will often have their budgets slashed by government, which may mean that authorities have to make cuts to services offered to the most vulnerable in society, which can include children with SEND (Weale, 2019). There have been many reports in recent times that the education of children with SEND is in crisis. The SEND ombudsman Michael King has told the BBC that 'parents are having to fight the system that was established to support them' (BBC, 2019). Two weeks later another report from a cross-party education commission stated that

> parents seeking support for children with SEND face unlawful practices, buck passing and a 'treacle' of bureaucracy. (Parliament UK, 2019b)

Roberts (2019), writing for *The Times Educational Supplement*, reports that organisations are calling for reform as they believe that the needs of children are not being properly met. In order to address these concerns, Gavin Williamson, the Education Secretary, has requested a major review of the support given to children with SEND (Gov.UK, 2019a). Only time will tell as to the effectiveness of this review and the implications it will have on the government itself, local authorities, and settings, not to mention the numbers of children and families who have to battle this out day in day out.

Both the EYFS and the SEND Code of Practice (DCSF, 2008; DFE and DOH, 2014) stress the importance of gathering evidence, which demonstrates how practitioners plan to support children's learning with both documents making use of the same cycle (Figure 4.1).

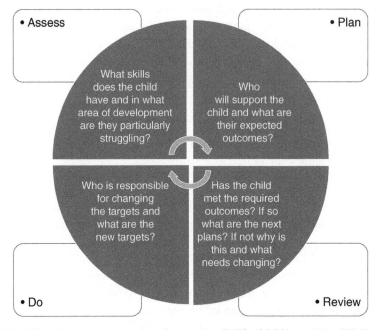

Figure 4.1   The planning cycle according to the EYFS (2008) and the SEND Code of Practice (2014)

Settings are also required to produce an informal plan for children that sets out the small steps that the setting is working on with the child concerned. These plans should be written collaboratively between the SENCO, key worker, parents and if possible the child, and should be reviewed termly.

REFLECTION

- Are you aware of the terms SEND support and the Education, Health and Care Plan?

- How do they both assist practitioners when working with children with SEND?

- What might be the challenges of both of these to children and their families?

The documents also discuss the role of the SENCO in supporting children with SEND. The newer Code of Practice (DFE and DOH, 2014) made some changes to the role of the SENCO, which were discussed in Chapter 2. Many settings, particularly those attached to schools, will employ their own SENCOs, but in private independent nurseries the local authority should employ SENCOs who will support settings (Crutchley, 2018).

Their role is to:

- gather information about all children who are either receiving SEN support or who may have an EHCP
- attend multi-agency meetings to discuss the children concerned
- discuss the child's progress with other professionals coming into the setting
- review the education plans which the children are working towards
- liaise with the child's key workers and parents about any concerns the child may have
- support any transitions that the child may experience
- organise any training needed by staff to support the needs of the children concerned (Revels, 2015).

PERSONAL NOTE 4.2

It is important to emphasise here that the application for an EHCP can be particularly stressful for parents. Whilst working as a Portage worker I supported many families who were involved in the process of applying for an EHCP. However, in order to ensure that a child is granted an EHCP, those writing the applications are encouraged to focus more on what the child cannot do rather than on what they can do. This means that parents need the support of practitioners who understand the system and can sensitively support parents through the process.

The final section of this chapter will consider the tools practitioners use to assess children and discuss the importance of the 'voice of the child' in assessment.

ASSESSMENT IN PRACTICE

OBSERVATIONS

In the main, observations are the main tool for summative assessment carried out by practitioners in settings. Cooper and Harlow suggest that observations are useful to

> watch / look at somebody and something and record what you have seen or just take in mentally what has been observed. (2018: 96)

There are, however, different types of observation that are used for different reasons.

NARRATIVE OBSERVATIONS

These are used to write down exactly what a child does in a particular given time span. They are a good tool to use to focus on the holistic development of the child and to ascertain the skills of the child as well as how they play socially, and to record how they communicate. The negative aspects of them are that it is sometimes hard to keep up with what the child is doing, and that they can be lengthy to complete and practitioners do not always have the time to focus on extensive observations. Also the child being observed may not want to be watched and may also try to draw the practitioner into what they are doing.

TIME SAMPLE OBSERVATIONS

The observations are carried out every five minutes for a given period of time. They give information relating to where the child likes to play and what they are interested in, their levels of engagement in an activity, their communication skills and their emotional wellbeing. The negative aspect of time sample observations is that in a busy setting where lots of activities are encouraged it may be hard to ascertain in short periods of time what the child is doing. These observations can be very useful when you might be recording the behaviour of children, as they could identify a particular time when a child/children will start to misbehave. For instance, they could demonstrate that the period before lunch is tricky for some children as they are starting to feel hungry, or the period before the setting closes can be difficult for some children. Using these observations can support practitioners who might be working with children who have behavioural issues:

- Antecedent – what happens before the child's outburst? Was it caused by some communication with another child? Does it always happen at the same time? Is a particular child/adult in the area when the child struggles?
- Behaviour – how did the child react? How did they demonstrate that they were angry?
- Consequence – what actions were taken after the outburst?

Settings can produce their own sheets to describe what happened and patterns may start to emerge as to why the child reacted like they did (Gloucestershire. Gov.UK, n.d.).

TRACKING OBSERVATIONS

Before tracking observations are carried out, a plan of the setting needs to be available with all the areas carefully plotted. The process will track how the children use the space, how long they spend on a certain activity and how well they focus on certain areas.

SNAPSHOT OBSERVATIONS

These are the briefest observations and they are usually logged on Post-it notes, which are then transferred to the child's learning-journey file. They are spontaneous moments in a child's life: they might be demonstrating something new that the child has done; it may be something that fulfils an area on the EYFS profile which can be logged; they may demonstrate a major achievement for a child. Sometimes a photograph will also be taken. The role of the practitioner is to record the development without any comment at all. I would also recommend logging any communication that the child may have made at the time.

LEARNING STORIES

These are similar to narrative observations but they record different aspects of the child. They focus on:

- the child's interests
- how involved in the activity they are
- how long they persist in the activity
- how they communicate
- how they take responsibility for what they are doing (Brodie, n.d.).

Learning stories are 'written as a story in the first person, as if the practitioner was talking to the child and explaining what they had observed' (p. 1).

These are the main types of observations carried out in settings, but there are other tools which focus more on the emotional wellbeing and their involvement in activities. One of these is Leuven scales. These measure on a scale from one to five the level at which a child engages in an activity:

Level 1 is extremely low so would indicate the child is not interested in the activity

Level 2 is low and demonstrates the child has some interest but does not engage for very long

Level 3 is moderate and although the child shows interest they may also look around the room at what others are doing

Level 4 is high where it is obvious that the child is enjoying the activity but they do not seem completely focused on it

Level 5 is high and this is where the child becomes completely engrossed in what they are doing (Royal College of Speech and Language Therapists, 2019).

Pen Green suggests that using the Leuven scale for children with SEND is helpful because it offers a different way of focusing on the observation of young children who perhaps cannot communicate orally or whose needs are so great that it is hard to ascertain their engagement in activities. It also keeps the child at the centre of all that they are doing (2018).

A more recent form of assessment has been added to those used in early years settings. This may be because of the prevalence of children with social and emotional issues in early childhood. The Early Intervention Foundation reported in 2015 that children from the age of three from deprived areas display poor social and emotional skills. If these are not addressed in settings, they could escalate even more. The new assessment tool is entitled 'Assessing Quality in Early Childhood Education and Care: Sustained Shared Thinking and Emotional Well-being (SSTEW) Scale for 2–5-year-olds provision'. This seeks to support children through sustained shared thinking in developing skills in emotional wellbeing; these in turn will support the child's ability to make friendships, use effective communication and support self-regulation.

DEVELOPMENTAL CHECKLISTS

We have already considered these earlier in the book. Discussion was made of the developmental checks that occur when children are age two. Whilst these are important for monitoring the progress of children's development, they can be problematic. Burman (2008) suggests that they can cause worry for parents, particularly if their children are not developing at the same level as other children, and that they can cause parents to think that their parenting is not 'good enough'. Some of the other pitfalls of these checklists are:

- children may not want to do the required activities when asked
- parents may not think it necessary to take their children for these – particularly if there are concerns about the development of the child
- not all children develop in the same way, so some areas of development may go along with the ages on the checklist whilst others fall behind.

It is important to note here that most early years settings use the Early Years Foundation Stage profile to monitor children in their care. However, the developmental bands in Development Matters are slightly wider and may be a better way to monitor children's progress.

REFLECTION ———————————————————

- Which of these methods of observing children do you have experience of?
- Do you think that there might be different ways for you to monitor children?
- What do you think are the benefits and challenges of them?

THE IMPORTANCE OF THE CHILD'S VOICE IN ASSESSMENTS

One of the most important factors that changed with the development of the new SEND Code of Practice (DFE and DOH, 2014) was the importance of listening to the child's voice. This gained more prominence in the early years as a result of the Every Child Matters document in 2003 produced by the New

Labour government, which was introduced in Chapter 1. One of the five outcomes of this document was that children should 'make a positive contribution' to matters that affect them (HM Government, 2003: 7). This means that they should be allowed to have a say in their own assessments. This can be problematic as many children with SEND also have difficulties with their communication. The term participation is often used to relate to the voice of the child and the necessity for them to be heard. However, this is seen by some as being controversial. Macblain et al. (2017) point out that views around the voice of the child may differ depending on who is being consulted. Some practitioners may struggle with the notion, suggesting that some children are not old enough to make big decisions in relation to their lives or they may struggle to communicate their views. MacNaughton et al. (2004) suggest that though children are considered able to make their own decisions, there is still 'contention' relating to children's 'meaningful participation' in issues that relate to them.

In Chapter 3 I referred to different ways in which children can be supported to communicate through Makaton, objects of reference, and the Picture Exchange Communication System (PECS) were introduced. All of these can support children to inform adults of their likes and dislikes, what activities they prefer and what parts of the setting they enjoy. Earlier in this chapter we focused on the use of observations to monitor children's progress, and learning stories would be particularly effective to use with children with SEND as they are compiled alongside the child, giving them a voice in their actions.

THE MOSAIC APPROACH

This approach is another programme which was especially designed for children in London by Clark and Moss (2001). It sought to give a voice to young children, particularly those who had special needs. The methods, which were first developed for use in research, were adapted and are now used to enable children to have a voice through different media. The approach views the role of the child as being central and an active participator in their own learning and exploration, using different tools to investigate their environments. Initially it was used with respect to the outdoor environment but it is now used in a range of settings to evaluate environments and ways of learning.

At the heart of the approach is the view that all children have a voice and also have a right to be heard and to be active in their own lives, but that this may be demonstrated through different formats rather than just relying on speech. In 2015 Rinaldi introduced the view that children have '1000 voices'. These different voices can be manifested in different ways such as via art, music, voice and movement. These voices are very much linked in the Mosaic approach.

The approach uses observations, child interviews and drawings, photographs, map making and tours of the setting. These are then followed by focus groups where the child explains their views to the adults involved (stage one). Secondly the data are discussed with all participants in a way that is acceptable to their needs (stage two). This enables a more in-depth analysis of the data. The third stage views implementation of the information gained during the process. This then becomes part of a continual reflective cycle which makes changes to the environment and ways of working in the light of what the research discovers (Borkett, 2018).

REFLECTION

- Do you recognise, as Rinaldi does, the many languages of children in your setting?
- Do you or could you use aspects of the Mosaic approach?
- Could you use some of these tools to enable children in your setting to use their 'hundred languages?'

THE USE OF AUGMENTATIVE COMMUNICATION STRATEGIES IN EARLY YEARS SETTINGS

The term augmentative communication refers to 'a set of tools and strategies that an individual uses to solve everyday communicative challenges' (Bailey, 2016: 1). These can be strategies similar to those mentioned in the final part of Chapter 2. The term refers particularly to strategies such as Makaton signs, Picture Exchange Communications System (PECS), Rebus symbols, and electronic communication systems that can be used either through touch or eye gaze. These systems can help to strengthen children's communication skills, with many of them incorporating speech alongside signs and symbols. All of these strategies not only help children who have special needs but can also support bilingual children who are learning English alongside another language. Whilst being bilingual is not a SEND in itself, some children from other cultures do struggle to learn more than one language (Borkett, 2018).

Bryan, a child born with cerebral palsy and brain damage, reports how he struggled to communicate at a young age and as a result spent much of his time in a special school being frustrated by his inability to communicate. Eventually his parents removed him from the school and they began to home educate him. They slowly discovered that with the use of an 'eye gaze' computer he was able to learn to read and subsequently communicate through the use of a mouse that worked when he looked at it. Bryan (2017) has since gone on to write a blog, which he uses to share his experience with other children with disabilities.

CASE STUDY 4.2

Robert

Robert was six years old and had cerebral palsy. Because of this some of his movements were slow and he had difficulty coordinating his mouth and tongue.

As a result of this his speech was quite difficult to understand. Robert had an older sister who loved to draw and colour and so he had grown up with pencils, crayons and felt tip pens and he too liked to use these to draw. Early on in his life these pictures seemed to represent things that he had done. At weekends he would take delight in drawing pictures that represented what he had done and these became a real tool for practitioners in his setting finding out what he did at home. Later on in Robert's life he had some emotional and mental health issues, and again his ability to draw what he was feeling helped to support his subsequent treatment.

Consider

- Have you ever considered that children's drawings can be a way in which they can have a voice?
- How might you use children's pictures to elicit their views?
- Are there any children who may struggle to draw their feelings?

Sometimes practitioners need to think differently about how they might give a voice to children who struggle to be heard.

As a result of reading this chapter you will have:

- understood how assessment is an integral part of educational practice and the links it makes to the curriculum
- discovered the importance of assessment in policy with particular emphasis on the Early Years Foundation Stage (EYFS) and the Special Educational Needs and Disability Code of Practice (SEND COP)
- considered the tools practitioners use to assess children and explored the importance of the 'voice of the child' in assessment.

The next chapter will discuss the importance of play for children in the early years and focus on some of the dilemmas and difficulties that children may experience if they have or are thought to have a SEND.

END OF CHAPTER QUESTIONS

- In what way has this chapter supported your understanding of the links between the curriculum and assessment?
- Having read this chapter do you think that children in the early years are aware that they are being assessed regularly?
- What do you see as being your role in assessing the development of young children?

FURTHER READING

Bryan, J. (2017) I talk with my eyes. *The Guardian.* www.theguardian.com/lifeand style/2017/jan/27/experience-i-talk-with-my-eyes

This is a really interesting newspaper article which is autobiographical and tells how someone who was thought to be unable to communicate was able to do so through a computer.

Clark, A. and Moss, P. (2011) *Listening to Young Children: The Mosaic Approach.* London: National Children's Bureau

This book introduces the reader to the Mosaic approach, a multi-method way of carrying out research with young children. The book describes the many and varied ways that children can do research and give their views on matters that affect them.

Early Education (2019) Getting it right in the EYFS means looking at the evidence. www.early-education.org.uk/getting_it_right_in_the-EYFS

This very recent piece of writing has been brought together by the Early Years Alliance – an organisation representing many charitable bodies who support the early years. It is a paper which sets out the concerns of many who see that the early years and particularly play is being eroded in favour of more 'school-based' subjects.

5

THE AMBIGUITIES OF PLAY

Chapter 3 focused on the importance of early intervention and discussed the value of a play-based curriculum. However, play can be a difficult concept for some children with SEND. This chapter focuses on the importance of play whilst recognising some of the dilemmas of this principle.

Through this chapter you will:

- understand why play and development are intrinsically linked, and understand barriers to this in terms of children with special educational needs and disabilities (SEND)

- explore some of the many theories that relate to child development and play with particular focus on the role of the practitioner

- consider how practitioners should support the play of children with SEND and introduce particular types of play that can support children with SEND.

This chapter will begin with a discussion around the notion of play as a tool to support children's early development and the benefits of this, whilst also acknowledging some of the barriers to a play-based curriculum in the light of a 'standards-driven' educational system and the fact that children with SEND may play differently. The chapter will then go on to introduce some of the many child development theories that particularly discuss the role of the adult in being pivotal in planning, facilitating and supporting play. It will finally discuss certain kinds of play that are useful when working with children with SEND, with particular emphasis on sensory play.

HOW ARE PLAY AND DEVELOPMENT LINKED IN EARLY CHILDHOOD?

In Chapter 1 various policies were introduced which particularly focused on the legislative needs of children with SEND. The Early Years Foundation Stage (EYFS) (DCSF, 2008) and the United Nations Convention on the Rights of the Child (UNCRC) (UNICEF, 1989) were both introduced. These discuss the importance of play for all children, and suggest that children learn best through play experiences that are well planned and delivered by practitioners who firstly have a good knowledge of child development and secondly are able to plan and facilitate play. The EYFS states that:

> children's play reflects their wide ranging and various interests and pre-occupations. In their play children learn at their highest level. Play with peers is important for children's development. (DCSF, 2008)

Through every edition of the EYFS play continues to be endorsed as the most appropriate way for young children to learn. The EYFS makes the case that all children are competent learners from birth and are rich in potential. It goes on to state that play should be at the heart of the delivery of the EYFS and that through play children have opportunities to explore inside and out in order to develop and learn. The document also states the need for practitioners to be able to plan and deliver play activities that are bespoke to every child, and take into account their interests, fascinations and ways of learning.

Alongside the EYFS, the Characteristics of Effective Learning (Early Education, 2012a), which were introduced in Chapter 1, support practitioners in the planning and implementation of activities. Both documents support the principle that children learn best through play irrespective of their needs, culture, gender, religion or home language. As with the EYFS, it states that children are born ready to learn and to explore, but also makes the case that development is not an automatic process. It suggests that if a child is given an environment that supports exploration and discovery, and builds positive relationships with peers and knowledgeable adults, the child will learn to play and therefore develop.

The UNCRC states in Article 31:

Every child has the right to relax, play and take part in a wide range of cultural and artistic activities. (UNICEF, 1989)

The International Play Association extends Article 31 by suggesting that play gives satisfaction to children, allows them to communicate and helps them to develop physically, emotionally and socially. It states that play 'is a means of learning to live and not merely a passing of time'. Although the Special Educational Needs Code of Practice (SEND CoP) (DFE and DOH, 2014) does not endorse the importance of play, it does extol the benefits of Portage, which was mentioned in Chapter 3. This home-based early intervention programme uses play to support and build children's development (www.portage.org.uk/about/what-portage). The fact that it is mentioned within government policy may suggest that learning through play is a recognised benefit for all children. However, currently in many early years settings practitioners are becoming concerned that the notion of play is being eroded by government officials who do not seem to value how essential it is for young children. Lewis (2017) states that in his view play is being reduced due to health and safety concerns and curricula, policy and ideology demanding that children should be taught about phonics, literacy and numeracy instead of being able to play.

WHAT IS PLAY?

As has been seen with many of the principles and concepts introduced in this book, play is yet another that is hard to describe or to define. Thompson (2019) discusses the difficulties of trying to identify play, suggesting that people's own experiences (of play) will have an impact on their views. Froebel, an early child development pioneer, viewed play as being 'the highest phase of child development' (Early Education, n.d.: 5), adding that play should never be trivialised, and that it can be used as a 'universal remedy' to a child's development. However Ailwood (2003) airs a precautionary note, suggesting that the West's preoccupation with children developing in ages and stages may mean that practitioners can become so anxious about noting children's development that they forget to engage in supporting children's play when needed.

As Borkett (2018) suggests, play is something that should be enjoyable and rich in resources and, as Bruce (2011) agrees, should enable a child to 'wallow in' and explore what things are and how they can be used, and help them to understand themselves and their identity. Thompson (2019) says that play should be 'intrinsically motivated by the child', which implies that the child should want to lead the play and that it should be more of a 'process' rather than requiring an end product (p. 134). Similarly Burman (2008) views play as being voluntary, enjoyable and self-directed, and notes that play should also support children's emotional wellbeing (p. 263). Sutton-Smith views play as offering children the ability to experience a range of emotions including frustration, achievement, disappointment and confidence and that through practice children can learn to manage these feelings. (2003: 6)

The International Play Association (2010) stresses that giving children time to play is a vital requirement of childhood, viewing it as a time for children to gain freedom, to amuse and to develop new skills. From all of these descriptions it can be determined that play is seen by many as a vital ingredient in a young child's development and learning. However, Grieshaber and McArdle (2010) make the case that play can privilege certain groups of children, and has the power to omit children who may have SEND or come from different cultures.

REFLECTION

- Write your own definition of play – how easy was it to define such a wide and complex principle?

- What do you see are the values of children learning through play?

- Have you ever experienced children being omitted from play for any particular reason?

CASE STUDY 5.1

A visit to Ghana

A few years ago I accompanied a group of 30 students who were all studying an Early Childhood Studies Degree to Ghana for three weeks. The country's educational department had introduced a new early years curriculum which focused more on the concept that children learn through play. While we were there we delivered some training to around 300 practitioners and then the students spent time in settings, trying to initiate the new curriculum with the practitioners.

One of the places that we visited was a children's home where many of the children had SEND. In parts of Africa there is a high incidence of children with disabilities, many of whom are abandoned by their parents and left outside to die. These children had then been collected by the police and taken to children's homes. The parents view disability as linked to witchcraft and therefore do not want the children growing up in their homes. The homes then take over the education of these children.

The home we went to was sparse, with just four bedrooms that the children shared. There was a lot of space outside where the children would play with each other but there were no toys anywhere. There was also a classroom where some of the children who were able to be educated had lessons from a teacher. These were very much based around writing and numbers.

We took into the home pots of bubbles, chalks, books, paper and some Lego. The children seemed to love our visits and particularly enjoyed the bubbles and drawing with the chalk outside. However, each day when we visited we would find the resources locked up in a cupboard – the practitioners did not seem to see the value of the activities.

Other students in different settings had the same experiences and we began to wonder why this was – despite the conference we had spoken at, the practitioners did not seem to understand what we were saying.

However, each weekend we went on trips to different parts of the country and experienced seeing abject poverty all around us. I slowly started to understand that for children in Africa education becomes a route out of poverty, and I think this is why practitioners and parents alike are so reluctant to encourage children to play. We continued to try to make gentle changes whilst also respecting their long-held views, and did see some change in the three weeks we were there. Only time will tell what changes may happen over the next few years.

Consider

- Have you ever seen childcare in a different country?

- What differences did you experience?

- What was your view on these differences?

WHAT ARE SOME OF THE CHALLENGES OF PLAY FOR CHILDREN WITH SEND?

It is important to establish here that for some children play can be a challenge. It may be difficult for children with SEND to communicate how they would like to lead their play, or indeed they may not understand the use of toys and therefore need practitioners to model or facilitate play which they may then copy. Moyles (2015) endorses the view that play 'is central to children's development' (p. 15) and that it has a significant role in brain development, thus underlining the view that all children should play. However, for some children this is difficult for the reasons mentioned previously. Batorowicz et al. (2016) carried out research in order to discover how children who use communication aids have power over their play. These children, who had severe physical difficulties and used the aids to communicate with peers and practitioners, were compared to 'normally functioning' young children. The study discovered that the children using these aids, when given the opportunity to play, were less able to give instructions to adults and that it took them longer to communicate.

In 2015 Blunkett and Rogers carried out research that investigated the play experiences of families who had a child with multiple needs – for instance they may be physically disabled and have difficulties with their communication and cognitive skills. Both researchers view play as being an invaluable way of learning for all children, acknowledging it as an opportunity particularly for children with SEND to learn alongside their non-disabled peers. However, the research unearthed many difficulties for the children with SEND and their families.

These included:

- limited local authority funding for playgrounds that are accessible for all children
- a lack of awareness of the training needs of practitioners working with children with SEND
- recognition that some children with SEND may need more support in settings to encourage them to play
- better strategic planning is needed in settings that have large numbers of children with SEND.

Godley and Runswick-Cole (2010) suggest that too often play is used as a 'diagnostic tool' (p. 500) for children with SEND that will move them on in their development. Thompson et al. (2019) suggest that the interest in play-based therapies such as Portage, discussed in Chapter 3, is grounded in developmental psychology – a system that focuses too much on the intellectual and cognitive changes that occur as people move through their lifespan. It is maybe fitting here to recognise that different professionals will view play differently. For instance:

- a social worker may see play as being a way of finding out about the social/emotional needs of a child or identifying a specific traumatic episode
- an educationalist will see play as being the way that children develop and learn
- a play worker will recognise that other elements of play are just as important such as where the play takes place, what resources the child uses; they view play as something natural which needs little intervention from adults
- a physiotherapist will see play as a fun way for a child to do physical exercises, which will support their holistic development
- a speech and language therapist may see play as encouraging children to use sounds and words to express themselves.

The above clearly demonstrates that practitioners can all have differing views of the role of play in a child's life. The EYFS makes the case that children should have experience of both adult-led play activities and activities they initiate themselves (DFE, 2017). McInnes et al. (2011) discovered in a study that practitioners' views on the importance of play as a tool for learning can depend on various factors:

- their level of qualification and the extent to which they have been taught the value of a play-based curriculum
- their own confidence in understanding the benefits of play to young children
- their ability to join in and encourage children to play.

Pellegrini and Blatchford (2002) suggest that child-initiated play is often overlooked or 'eroded' in settings across England and Europe by a standards-driven educational system more concerned with developmental checklists or Post-it notes that track the development of children. Atkinson et al. (2017), who carried out research with educational psychologists investigating the extent to which children with SEND were given the right to play in settings, identified that children with SEND were just one of many groups of children who were identified as 'at risk' when offered a play-based pedagogy. Children who often struggle to play, the authors found, included:

- those from other cultures
- those with social and emotional difficulties
- children with sensory impairments
- children with medical needs and extreme allergies.

Whilst researching this chapter I came across an article that suggests that play is the 'universal language' of childhood (2016: 302) and this made me think, as I had never considered this view before. Boucher et al. (2016) go on to endorse the case that all children have a right to play, and suggest that it is even more important for children with SEND and, in the case of their article, children with life-limiting illnesses. They state the case that play should be even more important for children in these circumstances as it improves their social and emotional wellbeing and is enjoyable. As they suggest, play should become 'golden nuggets' in a child's life.

PLAY IN THE WEST

It is pertinent here to note that the principle of play in the western world is very different from play in the developing world as the previous case study suggested. The developed world, which includes Europe, Australia, New Zealand, America and Canada, only makes up 18% of the world's countries. This means that for the remaining 82% of the world there is less focus on a play-based curriculum (Borkett, 2018).

The following case study demonstrates the dichotomies of a play-based curriculum for a family coming to the UK from Nigeria.

CASE STUDY 5.2

Akoye

Akoye was a year old when his parents left their country of origin in Africa due to the ongoing war. The family came to live in a city in the north of the UK. He was an only child and because of his parents' culture was much revered because he was a boy.

When the family signed up to their local GP surgery the doctor shared his concerns that Akoye's development was not progressing as well as expected. Akoye was referred to the local children's centre to be seen by the Portage team there. His parents struggled to see that there was anything amiss with Akoye and believed that his development was delayed due to the atrocities he had witnessed before they left Africa.

(Continued)

The Portage worker started working with the family and began to track Akoye's development. However, when she explained to the family that she would be using play to support Akoye's development they became unhappy. One of the reasons they had fled to the UK was because of its educational system, which they believed was far superior to that of their home country. They wanted Akoye to learn to read and write rather than learning through play.

Visits began, and very slowly Akoye started to respond to the activities suggested. As well as this progress the worker developed a good relationship with Akoye's family. She did not want to dismiss the parents' wishes for Akoye to learn to read and write so she began including a book at each visit, and she also recommended that his family should share books with Akoye in between visits. She also, when his physical skills allowed, introduced mark-making activities, explaining to his parents that this was a precursor to him being able to write. Through these sensitive changes the Portage worker was able to comply with Akoye's parents' wishes but also indicate how play can support further academic activities as Akoye grows.

Consider

- What are the benefits of working with families from different cultures?

- Have you ever had to change practice to support the cultural views of families? If so, what was the result of these changes?

- Have you ever considered the importance of culture in a child's life?

The first part of this chapter has recognised that whilst play is accepted by many to be something that all children can do, there are also many barriers and challenges to play. The chapter will now go on to discuss some of the child development theories that, in the main, promote the important role of the practitioner in supporting children's play, particularly for those children who have SEND.

CHILD DEVELOPMENT THEORIES THAT ARE LINKED TO PLAY

FREDRICH FROEBEL

Froebel was born in Germany in 1782 and was an educator. He invented the word kindergarten, which is still used across the world to define settings. It was Froebel's belief that through experience children build their ideas and views of the world. He was very much against splitting development into categories, believing instead that all learning is linked. Froebel developed the term 'gifts', which relates to blocks of wood still seen in many early years settings across the world, and 'occupations', these being resources such as sticks, clay, slates, chalk, wax, etc. Froebel first developed the term 'open-ended play', which defines play that children engage in for play's sake and not for any end product.

In terms of practitioners, Froebel believed that their role was to carefully observe the play of children and to try to understand that play and how it linked to a child's development.

MARIA MONTESSORI

Montessori was born in 1870 in Italy. She became a doctor and went on to work with children, many of whom had SEND. She held the view that children learn differently and at their own pace, whilst recognising all children as active learners who were self-motivated to play. She believed that children have different ways of learning, and made the case that children should receive an education that is particularly suited to their needs, fascinations and preferred ways of learning. Montessori particularly focused on the environment and resources available to children and the ways that they interacted with these. She stressed the importance of what she called 'sensorial impressions', which enable children to experiment and learn. In Montessori settings children are not split into particular age groups, which enables children with SEND to learn from their peers and adults in the group. At the beginning of Montessori's work with children she promoted the outside as being an area where children could explore and learn.

The role of the practitioner in Montessori settings is to sit back and observe the child well and to ensure that the play offered is well planned and specifically relates to what fascinates the child. This is a similar view to that held in settings today – that practitioners begin with observations of the child, noting their fascinations, interests and ways of learning and using these to then plan different ways of working that will help the child to develop further.

LEV VYGOTSKY

Vygotsky was a Russian psychologist, philosopher and teacher who was born in 1896. At this time child development was just emerging as a field of interest. Vygotsky believed that both the child's cultural environment and their social world had an impact on their cognitive skills. He believed that very young children learnt best through play and he observed a link between children's communications skills and their ability to learn. He recognised the importance of the adult as being crucial to a child's learning and developed the view that children do not develop in a bubble but that the things and people around them will also support their development.

One of Vygotsky's most famous areas of work is the zone of proximal development (ZPD). This relates to the support that a practitioner or a child's peers may give a child at the start of learning a new skill, which is slowly removed as the child becomes more proficient in learning the skill independently (Thompson, 2019). This is a crucial role in the work of practitioners who particularly work with children with SEND and who may need to give more support to children's development and learning.

GOLDSCHMIED

Elinor Goldschmied was born in 1910 and was educated at home. Like Montessori, she was fascinated with playing outside as a child. She liked nothing more than using everyday materials she found in her home to play with. As one of seven children this may have made good economic sense too. Goldschmeid liked playing with mud, water, stones, sticks and leaves. When she grew up she went to the Froebel Institute to train to become what we would now call an early years teacher. The Froebel Institute fostered her love and enthusiasm of using everyday activities to explore and learn from. In 1946 Goldschmeid went to live in Italy, where she worked in an institution for children who had been abandoned and were born out of marriage (something that was scorned in those days). She was deeply moved by these children, who she saw as being 'closed off' and afraid of any kind of human contact. She started to offer the children objects from the environment, such as stones, shells, small pieces of wood and fabric, in a wicker basket. Slowly the children began to respond to these and to the adults who would interact with them (Hughes, n.d.). These treasure baskets are still used across the UK and offered to babies and the youngest children.

Treasure baskets are a wonderful resource for children with SEND, who often gain a lot from what is now called sensory play. The choice of activities may need to be limited to begin with so that children are not overstimulated by too many items, but often children can concentrate and enjoy manipulating these products over time.

The role of the practitioner here is to simply observe the child, focusing on which objects they prefer, how they use them and ensuring that the resources are safe. The observations made are then used to inform future resources used in the baskets in relation to what fascinates the child.

CASE STUDY 5.3

Peter

Orr (2003), who for many years was the head teacher of a school for children who were blind and visually impaired, wrote about a child named Peter who attended his school. Peter was born blind in the early 1950s and had other cognitive and physical needs. He loved nothing better than sitting in his old enamel bath at home with an abundance of household items which he enjoyed banging against the side of the bath. Gradually he learnt that the different materials made different noises and felt different. He often discarded those made from plastic, preferring the metallic clanging noise of metal and the smooth feel of wood. His father then drilled holes into the bath and placed different utensils on a chain, making what we might now describe as a 'treasure basket'. As Peter's fine motor skills developed, different articles were added to the bath in order that his parents and SEND support worker were able to observe how he related to the textures of them.

As Peter grew he also used to enjoy sitting in a wicker laundry basket – seemingly feeling secure within the slightly raised edges which held him there. His parents quickly discovered that the things he liked to touch the most were those made from smooth wood, and he would touch and feel these for long periods of time. It is important to note here that for children with visual impairments who may well go on to learn Braille, a system children use to read and write with, exercises that develop their capacity to touch different textures are vital. Children who are blind will use their fingertips to identify the tiny raised dots which form the letters of the alphabet in Braille. Peter loved any opportunity to feel different textures and he also liked to play with his sister's very long hair, which he loved weaving through the basket – much to her disapproval.

This is an example of an early day treasure basket which would have been introduced a while before they became popular in early years settings. The case study indicates the need for children with SEND to be given sensory activities.

Consider

- Could you try making a treasure basket?

- Have you ever used treasure baskets or everyday objects to support children's learning?

- How important are sensory activities to your practice?

JEROME BRUNER

Bruner was born in the United States of America in 1915 and like Vygotsky was a psychologist. Bruner views all children as being active in their own learning whilst acknowledging that they need first-hand experiences to develop their learning and knowledge of the world. Bruner also placed great emphasis on the way that adults can support children's learning, viewing them as 'instruments' who share their knowledge of both the level of a child's development and also the way that the child prefers to learn (Borkett, 2018). Bruner discusses the term 'scaffolding', which Daniels and Taylor (2019) describe as being 'where the teacher extends a child's learning by focusing on the skill to be acquired' (p. 52). It is perhaps useful to view this as you would the scaffolding on a building which supports the building to stay up and is removed once the structure is secure. Another element of the child's life that was important to Bruner was the culture of the child. Bruner believed, as does Moyles (2015), that the cultural heritages that children demonstrate through their play bring with them to a setting the opportunity for all children to 'be unique' (DCSF, 2008). Both Vygotsky and Bruner are socio-constructivists who see the social world of the child as an essential part of their learning.

BARBARA ROGOFF

Rogoff, a more contemporary theorist, was born in 1950 and is an educationalist who – unlike Bruner and Vygotsky – focuses less on the science of how children learn and more on how children learn through their interactions, culture, cultural tools and ways of being (Borkett, 2018). Rogoff (2003), who is very interested in how children from other cultures learn, uses the term 'guided participation' in a similar way to Vygotsky's ZPD and Bruner's scaffolding. However, rather than viewing the support given to young children as solely the responsibility of practitioners, Rogoff stresses the importance of the wider family, elders and faith leaders in supporting young children to learn new skills. This view is akin to the view of Bronfenbrenner discussed in Chapter 3, who believes that each part of a child's family is linked in some way.

IN SUMMARY

There are similarities and differences between these theories. All of them value play as being important and enjoyable to all children. If we examine the work of Froebel, Montessori and Goldschmied we see similarities in their views about the use of natural resources in children's play. We have seen that Goldschmied's views were formed from her Froebelian training, and in many settings across the country, and indeed the world, natural resources are used to encourage children to learn and, more importantly, to have fun as they learn.

Another thing that is interesting with these first three theorists is the value that they place on the role of the practitioner in observing children's play. Their views are less about practitioners' interaction and more about the facilitating of the play. By that I mean setting up the resources, ensuring that the environment is attractive and enticing, and – importantly – ensuring that the resources are safe. They also focus on the importance of practitioner observations. These observations should both give an account of the actions and fascinations of children through their play and be used to plan future activities (DCSF, 2008).

However Bruner, Vygotsky and Rogoff value the role of children's peers and knowledgeable practitioners to support their development and learning. They view practitioners as being essential to a child's learning and suggest different but very similar ways to support children's play. Rogoff moves this view on by suggesting that the role of the adult should not just be the priority of practitioners but should include all adults involved in the life of the family and child.

REFLECTION

- How important do you view the role of the practitioner to be in a child's play?
- Do you see the adult as more of an observer, a facilitator or somebody who engages with that play?
- Do you believe that there is a danger in the adult becoming too involved in the play of children?

THE PRACTITIONER'S ROLE IN SUPPORTING PLAY

Bruce (2003), whilst recognising that adults are important in terms of supporting children's play, makes the case that too often they intervene too much and this means that the notion of child-led play is lost. If one goes along with the view of the UNCRC (UNICEF, 1989) that all children have a right to play, perhaps practitioners need to intervene less and enable children to lead play in their own inimitable way. This is a view shared by Fisher (2016), whose book entitled *Interacting or Interfering?* makes the case that practitioners should sometimes intervene and support children's play, but should also sit back and observe those 'golden nuggets' of play which demonstrate independent learning. However, maybe that would mean that children end up playing differently from the way that adults expect them to. McInnes et al. (2011) make the case that practitioners can have different understandings of the role of play in children's development and that this can affect how they view play and whether it is beneficial to young children.

PERSONAL NOTE 5.1

One of the most important elements of practice that I learnt as a Portage worker when working with children with SEND was the necessity of breaking tasks down into tiny steps. I likened the role of Portage worker to Mary Poppins, who would come along with her bag full of interesting resources and toys. Firstly I would focus essentially on the skills the child already had and then focus on the developmental level they were currently working on. The targets for the child would always be chosen alongside the parents' wishes and would encourage children to learn skills that would often seek to encourage language. Once these had been determined, the targets would be broken down into tiny steps – a bit like the scaffolding that Bruner referred to.

Two activities that could always be found at the bottom of my bag were a pot of bubbles and a soft ball, both of which were fun and an invaluable part of my work. During each visit there would be a mix of activities – first the ones that were focused on the developmental needs of the child, and then there would be a longer period of child-initiated play. During this time I would give the child the opportunity to explore their choice of activities from the bag. Most children chose either the ball or the bubbles. Gradually, as the child became more aware of what both toys did, I would initiate little games such as 'ready, steady go', either blowing the bubbles or rolling the ball to the child before the word go. As the child became more accustomed to the activity they might initiate the word go in some way – this might be through a look, an utterance or eye pointing. As time went on the children would, if they were able, say the word; others may not use the word but may sign it if using Makaton, and others may make their own utterance if they were non-verbal. These small, inexpensive toys supported the children's communication and cognitive abilities immensely. By giving children the choice of activity they were able to input into what happened during the sessions.

ENVIRONMENTS FOR INCLUSION AND LEARNING

When planning for children's play it is important that their bespoke needs, interests and fascinations are central to the activities chosen. This indeed can be a challenge if there are a large number of children in the setting. However, some activities will be a daily occurrence and many would be considered as being sensory activities which, because of their ability to stimulate the brain, are fundamental to the development of all children (Gascoyne, 2013). Emmons and Anderson (2005) agree, stating that sensory experiences are vital for a child with SEND. Gascoyne (2012) made the case that the brain needs sensory stimulation for it to develop, ascertaining that children with SEND in particular need an environment rich in sensory experiences.

Often these are the activities that children with SEND are drawn to, so it is important that they have access to lots of sensory activities, such as:

- sand
- water
- gloop or cornflour
- finger painting
- playdough, which might have scent or glitter added to it.

However, it is worth noting that children on the autistic spectrum can have difficulties with some sensory activities, so these do need planning with the particular child in mind. Sometimes a child with autism may behave in a way that you wouldn't immediately link to sensory sensitivities. They may be unable 'to deal with everyday sensory information which can cause sensory or information overload' (National Autistic Society, 2016b).

TREASURE BASKETS

As well as the activities listed above, as we read earlier in the case study relating to Peter, treasure baskets are sometimes available for children with SEND. They are baskets of natural resources which children can finger, mouth, touch and smell. A treasure basket might include the following:

- wooden pegs
- large stones
- wooden spoons
- natural sponges
- large buttons
- pieces of fabric.

The practitioner will give the child the basket of objects and watch what they do with the resources. It is recommended that practitioners do not engage with the children's play, but, as Dowling (2006) postulates, when working with children with SEND they may need the play to be modelled by an adult as children with SEND sometimes need more interaction with adults and can also struggle with the concept of play.

CASE STUDY 5.4 ————————————————

Alexa

Alexa was 18 months old when I started visiting her. She had general developmental delay which affected each part of her learning. She particularly loved playing with noisy toys, dolls and inset jigsaw puzzles. Because of Alexa's syndrome she put objects to her mouth a lot. She seemed to gain satisfaction from this and her mother accepted this as part of her condition. Alexa made a lot of progress over time and when she was two and a half her mother started looking at nurseries for her to attend. She was keen that she should go to her local nursery, where she would meet children from her own community. The nursery chosen welcomed children with special needs and so were happy to give her a place.

One afternoon just after Alexa started I went and visited her there. She was happily playing alongside other children and trying to communicate with them. Although she was then able to walk she was still a little wobbly, but this did not seem to affect her physically moving around the nursery. She particularly liked being outside and playing on the large wooden equipment with the help and encouragement of her key worker.

On this particular day, when she had finished on the equipment she went over to a sensory area where there were cones, acorns and glass pieces (like you might put in a vase) in large wooden boxes for the children to either finger or put into pots. I noticed that Alexa was putting these into her mouth and I became alarmed. There had been times in the past when Alexa had swallowed small stones and I was concerned that she might do this with the glass beads. I asked her key worker if the pieces could be removed when Alexa was there and she said she would ask the manager of the setting. I did warn Alexa's Mum and hoped that this would be the end of the incident. However, the school was not prepared to dispense with the glass beads because they felt it would impede the other children's enjoyment of them if they were removed.

Consider

- What would you do in this circumstance?
- Do you hold a similar view?
- How could the setting have dealt with this situation in a more inclusive way?

IMAGINATIVE PLAY

Other types of play that are important for children would be imaginative play areas. These can be used to encourage children to 'act out' what goes on in their homes. This can support them to make sense of their world as well as encourage communication and social opportunities for them (Brock et al., 2009). These are important for all children but even more so for children with SEND, whose communication may be less well developed. In these areas dressing-up play can be encouraged. It has been suggested by some that imaginative play activities are vital in order for children to develop their language skills (Weisberg et al., 2013).

This is an area of play where children might need the support of adults by the latter getting alongside the children and facilitating their play. This would not mean taking it over but playing alongside the children, helping to support their own self-initiated play. Many practitioners, including myself, will have fond memories of the opportunities to play alongside children: being the patient while the children are doctors or nurses, or being the child whilst the child acts out the teacher's role. These opportunities are enjoyable for all concerned and can be amazing opportunities to model language.

SMALL-WORLD PLAY

These play activities, which might include Lego, Duplo, dolls' houses, garages, are also an important aspect of play and may be another area that children with fine motor difficulties may struggle with. Again, adults are sometimes needed to assist the play without taking it over. Some children with autism can struggle with these types of play as they may be unable to imagine how the figures in this kind of activity may think and react. They may also struggle to play alongside other children or take turns with them. However, a knowledgeable adult who knows the child well can support a child's play and their understanding of the world. I have also used large dolls' houses to support children's social and emotional wellbeing, especially those who live in unstable environments. Children living in chaotic households where there are tears and shouting may use such activities to act out what has gone on at home, particularly if there are safeguarding concerns.

OUTDOOR PLAY

For children with SEND the opportunities for playing outside are endless. Spending time outdoors gives children the chance to be free from the constraints of being inside and can enable them to engage more in larger physical play, whether this be by running freely or by climbing on good-quality wooden climbing frames. Brewer (2016) believes that being outside can alleviate anxiety for children with SEND, whilst better supporting the development of social skills.

By reading this chapter you will have:

- understood why play and development is intrinsically linked and understand barriers to this in terms of children with SEND
- explored some of the many theories that relate to child development and play with a particular focus on the role of the adult
- considered particular types of play that are useful for children with SEND with a particular emphasis on sensory play.

The next chapter will consider the importance of working alongside the families of children with SEND.

END OF CHAPTER QUESTIONS

- How has this chapter supported your knowledge of play and its importance for children with SEND?

- Do you think that practitioners need to utilise different approaches to play for children with SEND?

- How might you make changes to the environment to ensure that children with SEND are better able to access play activities?

FURTHER READING

Blunkett, D. and Rogers, L. (2015) *Making the Case for Play.* London: Sense. www.sense.org.uk/play

This publication discusses some of the challenges and ambiguities of play for children with SEND.

Goodley, D. and Runswick-Cole, K. (2010) Emancipating play: Dis/abled children, development and deconstruction. *Disability & Society* 25 (4): 419–512.

This journal article discusses what play is and how it relates to children with SEND, especially when it is used so much as a teaching tool.

Thompson, P. (2019) Supporting play. In: Fitzgerald, D. and Maconochie, E. (eds) *Early Childhood Studies – A Student's Guide.* London: Sage.

This chapter discusses many of the theories of play and child development, and focuses on the need for children to be able to learn through their own self-initiated play.

6

PARTNERSHIPS WITH PARENTS AND FAMILIES

This chapter focuses on the importance of working closely with the parents and carers of children with SEND.

By the end of this chapter you will:

- know something of the historical concept of working alongside families when children have special educational needs and disabilities (SEND)

- begin to understand how parents may relate to the diagnosis and 'label' of a particular SEND/medical condition

- consider how relationships within the family can be affected when a child has SEND, particularly in relation to the siblings.

As with many of the chapters in this book, the beginning of this one will focus on historical legacies of policy and theorists relating to the value of working alongside parents. This is always important but takes on a deeper meaning if the family has a child with SEND, as the support given may differ greatly from that offered when working with parents who have a 'normally developing' child. The chapter will then consider how parents may feel when their child/ren receive a 'label' of a particular disability, either immediately after birth or later on in their lives. There will also be some discussion relating to aspects of grief that parents may experience when they first suspect that their child has a SEND, or when they receive the 'label' for that disability. Finally the chapter will discuss how disability can affect the whole family, including the siblings of children with SEND.

In order to gain an honest picture of the role of parents I have asked two sets of parents to support the writing of this chapter. Alongside them, an early years practitioner has also shared her wisdom of the importance of working alongside parents. Their views will be added throughout the chapter.

THE HISTORICAL NOTION OF WORKING ALONGSIDE PARENTS

The need to work with parents has been an important element of the Early Years Foundation Stage (EYFS) since its inception in 2008 and since then, whilst this requirement has remained, it has changed slightly depending on which political party has been in government. The newly revised EYFS 2019 suggests that the definition of a parent first introduced though the Education Act of 1996 still holds – that parents are:

- parents of a child
- any person who is not a parent of a child but who has parental responsibility for a child
- any person who has care for a child (Education Act 1996).

However, Ward suggests that these definitions of 'parent' may be outdated and only really focus on the understanding of 'parental responsibilities' (2010: 3). Weinberger et al. (2005) make the suggestion that the role of a parent has, as with the definition of the word family, changed greatly over the past 50 years and therefore this understanding is not as relevant now as it may have been when the Education Act was written in the 20th century.

The government suggests that a parent should:

- provide a home for the child whilst protecting and supporting them throughout their life
- be responsible for choosing where the child is educated
- be in agreement to any medical treatment that the child requires (Gov.UK, n.d. b).

These suggestions recognise how the role of the parent has changed and that it is not necessarily the biological parent who makes decisions in relation to education and a child's medical needs. The original EYFS made the case that 'parents are a child's first and enduring educator', going on to stress the requirement for early years settings to work alongside parents within a 'partnership'. However, the new EYFS maintains the need to:

- inform parents of a child's development in relation to Early Learning Goals (ELG) and the Characteristics of Effective Learning (COEL)
- share information with parents or other relevant adults
- build crucial relationships with parents that ensure that relevant information is shared.

So the role of working with partners still holds and, in my view, becomes even more essential when working with parents of children with SEND. Both SEND Codes of Practice (2001 and 2014) extol the need to work in close partnership with parents throughout the child's life, and discuss the need for parents' views about the education of their child to be listened to and acted upon.

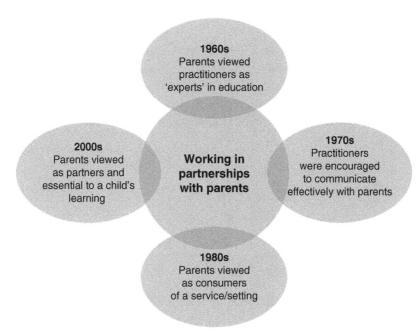

Figure 6.1   How parental responsibility has changed over the years

Adapted from Ward (2010: 33–34)

Figure 6.1 describes how partnerships with parents have changed over the last six decades. As with other concepts, these changes have arisen because of changes in society, policy and government.

REFLECTION ————————————————————

- Think back to when you were a child. How has support for parents changed since then?
- What are some of the essential components of working with families?
- What are some of the challenges of working in partnership with families?

THE ROLE OF THE PRACTITIONER IN WORKING WITH FAMILIES OF CHILDREN WHO HAVE SEND

Sheila Wolfendale (1993), an educational psychologist, focused her work around the necessity for early intervention in the home for children with SEND. Wolfendale also stressed the importance of parental partnership particularly in terms of the assessment of children with SEND, which was discussed in Chapter 4. She supported the Department for Education in writing the first Special Educational Needs Code of Practice in 2001 and was a great advocate for Portage and the support that this gave to both parents and their children. She firmly believed that it was vital for parents of children with SEND to be supported as early as possible and for that support to follow through a child's life until they went into education. She also advocated that support should be offered in all areas of the child's development. This means that the Portage worker also supports a family with the many clinical appointments:

- speech and language therapy
- audiology
- physiotherapy
- occupational health
- paediatricians
- educational psychologists

to name just a few.

Wolfendale viewed this support as vital to both the family and the Portage worker in terms of supporting the child's holistic development. It also meant that treatments suggested by other therapists could be incorporated into Portage sessions.

Another strong advocate for working alongside parents is Liz Brooker. Brooker was a reader at the Institute of Education in the UK and worked as a teacher before becoming a university lecturer. Liz carried out extensive ethnographic research with Bangladeshi communities in London (Brooker, 2016).

Through this she discovered the unique aspects of family life in these communities and exposed the nature of support that parents prefer (Borkett, 2018).

Brooker saw the need for hierarchies within staff teams to be dismantled and for the roles of practitioner, parent and child to be equal. She initiated a concept entitled the 'triangle of care'. This suggests that the three relationships between parent, practitioner and child should be equal (see Figure 6.2).

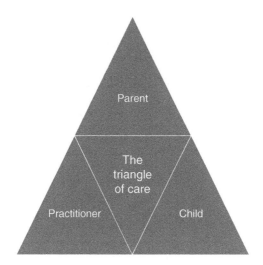

Figure 6.2 The triangle of care

Adapted from Brooker (2016)

However, it is my belief that when a child has SEND, whilst this diagram is relevant one should also note the significance of other professionals working with families. I therefore advocate that another triangle should be placed at the bottom of the original shape to make a diamond – at each point of this additional triangle would be therapists, educational personnel and family support workers. The lines joining these professionals should be broken as they may not be as significant as the first three (see Figure 6.3).

This newer model therefore ensures that all of the types of support that families receive are seen as essential aspects of their child's life and are provided in a more equal way.

In Chapter 3 the work of Urie Bronfenbrenner was introduced, and his theory very much relates to this chapter. He believes that the child and their families are within the microsystem – the first circle of his ecological systems theory. The second circle, known as the mesosystem, relates to other people who work with the family, which, in the case of children with SEND, may be the many other professionals considered within the diamond proposed in Figure 6.3.

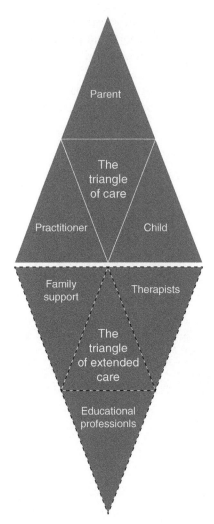

Figure 6.3   Multi-agency diagram

Adapted from Brooker (2016)

WORKING AS A TEAM

In Chapter 1 the Together from the Start document was introduced. This was seen at the time as groundbreaking as it sought to bring multi-agency profession-als together in a team, first called the 'team around the child' (TAC). The Children's Workforce Development Council stated the TAC was a 'model of multi-agency service provision' (2009: 6). The assigned lead worker would sup-port the parents to produce a detailed history of the nature of their child's disabilities, and this negated the need for parents to repeat the story of their child over and over again. Sadly this support has diminished with changes to government priorities. However the idea of multi-agency support is still there for children with SEND, and the meetings are now more focused on the 'team around the family' (TAF), thus suggesting that it is not just the child that needs support but the entire family.

Whilst these meetings are seen by some as essential, they can also produce negative emotions. Gibbs (2005) suggests that teachers and parents can feel 'vulnerable, anxious and may panic' as they are expected to speak about their child.

The people who I asked to support me through the writing of this chapter all stressed the importance of working as a team with all professionals involved, suggesting that this helps to ensure consistency, continuity and honesty. The practitioner explained that families are individual and will need different areas of support and at different times in a child's life. This might advocate that a baby born with a particular disability such as Down syndrome, cerebral palsy or spina bifida would need immediate support before they leave the hospital with their child. For others it might be later on in the child's life when there are concerns from family and other professionals of a possible diagnosis of some kind of SEND. Scope (n.d. a) suggest that after diagnosis parents may gain support from other parents who have been through a similar experience – they may read of others' experiences online through a blog or might join groups/charities for children with SEND. However, information online can also be challenging. Whatever the child's disabilities there will be different degrees of it that will affect each child in unique ways. A parent may well make positive/negative assumptions when reading information online or through books about the condition.

Whenever support is needed it is vital that parents are allowed a voice. They need to be confident that no question is too small, and as the EYFS recognises, they know their child the best and are aware of their needs. Kagan et al. (1999) suggest that the needs of parents who have children with SEND are not just confined to the early years but they go on through the child's school years and beyond. They also make the case that the financial cost of having a child with SEND is far greater, and although parents can receive benefits for the child, the benefits system 'alienates many parents from claiming the benefits they are entitled to' (p. 369).

MacNaughton and Hughes make the suggestion that at times practitioners can be guilty of 'homogenizing children' (2011: 6). This is when practitioners see certain groups of parents/children as all the same. An example of this would be when they think that all children on the autistic spectrum learn and behave in the same way, or they make an assumption that the support given to parents of children with SEND should be exactly the same, rather than seeing all parents as individuals with differing needs. Another term they use is 'silencing', which suggests that professionals can make parents feel that they are being excluded and not listened to. This could be in terms of not being given enough time to speak with practitioners to discuss their child's needs, or it may be in relation to the building or environment. For instance, a child with SEND may need more space to move around in if their physical skills are limited. They may need particular resources to support their development, or may need changing facilities.

If the setting does not acknowledge any of these needs then they may be guilty of 'silencing' that family.

REFLECTION

- What experience have you had of working with a team, either through work, study or volunteering?
- Have you ever experienced 'silencing' or homogenising of children in your settings?
- What are some of the benefits and challenges of working as a team?

Both parents who supported this chapter felt that whilst the ideals of multi-agency working were positive, the realities of it were a little more challenging. Maconochie and Branch recognise that when agencies work together to support children with SEND the health needs of the child improve. However they also acknowledge some of the challenges of working together, such as breakdowns in communication, the clarification of roles and responsibilities, and the need to gain the family's 'trust and mutual respect' (2018: 270). Both parents talked of the need to tell their 'child's story' over and over again. They discussed a lack of coordination between services, and one suggested that it was not until her daughter went to school that the services really 'kicked in'.

CASE STUDY 6.1

Joanne's story

Joanne was in her early twenties when she had her first child – a daughter called Sophie. Soon after Sophie was born she was found to have a slight heart defect and had to have a pacemaker put into her heart. Joanne felt that she was a listless baby who got very tired, but felt that this was probably due to her heart condition.

As Sophie got older she seemed to be slightly behind in her developmental milestones and Joanne and her husband started to wonder whether things were not quite right. Joanne discussed her concerns with her health visitor on numerous occasions. Joanne supported Sophie's development as best she could and took her to parent and baby groups and other services offered through her local Sure Start centre.

Sophie continued to meet her milestones, but each one of them was slightly later than the norm. After many changes of health visitor, one visited who Joanne felt really listened to her but still did not offer any kind of support to Joanne, who clearly recognised that something was amiss.

When Sophie was two and a half she was offered a place at her local nursery, which was attached to the school that she would attend. Staff there recognised that Sophie's development was slow but unfortunately did not seem to offer any kind of support. However, a change of staff in the nursery meant that the Special Educational Needs Co-ordinator (SENCO) became Sophie's teacher. She recognised Sophie's needs and gave Joanne the support that she needed in recognising those needs.

Recently Sophie received a diagnosis of autism. Joanne felt relieved that there was an obvious reason for the delays in her development, but felt angry that it had taken this long for the condition to be confirmed. Sophie continues to attend her small local primary school, but struggles with transitions and can become quite anxious if she does not understand what is expected from her or if routines in the setting change for any reason. Joanne, whilst keen to keep her in mainstream education, is mindful of the fact that whilst this school is keen to support Sophie in any way they can, this may not always be the case.

Consider

- How would you react if a parent told you that they suspected their child might have a SEND?
- What support would you put in place?
- How would you ensure that information was shared with other practitioners in a confidential, professional way?

The next section of this chapter will discuss the benefits and challenges of labels and the support that may be needed by parents when their child receives a label of a SEND.

THE DIAGNOSTIC AND 'LABELLING' PROCESS

Parents who have children with SEND will have often gone through a process of diagnosis. Many parents discuss the challenges of this and the need for them to be constantly fighting for their child. Nimmo (2019) describes the support processes that she needed to be in place to support her daughter who had significant learning difficulties. She states that at times she was 'her carer, her voice and her advocate', going on to describe how she had to learn to 'navigate' many systems of education, health and social care in order to get the support her family needed. For some parents this process begins during pregnancy as tests for disabilities are offered, such as a prenatal test that can now diagnose Down syndrome and spina bifida during pregnancy. The actress Sally Phillips, who has a son with Down syndrome, spoke candidly when a new antenatal test for the syndrome was introduced in 2016 (*The Guardian*, 2017). She stated that the threat of eugenics, which is described as being the 'testing of the foetus during pregnancy' for certain abnormalities related to disability, was advocating 'selective breeding to determine the future of society'. Nelson (2016) discusses the fact that eugenics is not a modern-day concept, explaining that Galton began discussions on this in 1883. Modern-day proponents of eugenics state that it can support parents to make an informed choice relating to whether they abort their child and it also supports families before their child is born in accessing important information on their child's disability. Clinicians also report that these tests can ensure that early intervention, such as that discussed in and after Chapter 3, can be put into place immediately when the child is born (Coffey, 2013). This is one of those difficult ethical discussions that readers of this book will have differing views on.

Other parents may be grappling with an anxious voice in their head questioning whether or not their child's development is as it should be, or whether there is something amiss. In this case it may take longer for the family to be given a diagnosis of SEND. As we saw in Joanne's case in the previous section, it can take many years of fighting before the child is granted that diagnosis. This might be because there is a lack of information relating to the child and the difficulties they are having. It may be because of a lack of financial resources which are currently stripping local authorities of the cash to support families (Runswick-Cole, 2019). It can also be that the nature of the disability is so unusual that a diagnosis is not easy to give. One parent said they had to wait until their child was a teenager before they knew what disability she had.

Whatever the situation of the child when a diagnosis is made, there are many advantages and disadvantages to the child being given a judgement of a particular SEND. However, before these are discussed, it is important to consider the impact of this process on both the parents and the children. If the child has been born with a disability, whether or not the parents knew about this during pregnancy, there will be a period of time when they have to come to terms with the fact that their child is not as they were expecting. Relatives may not know how to support the new family, and may fail to recognise that whatever the needs of the child, they have still welcomed a new child into the family and this is reason for celebration (White, 2017).

When a diagnosis comes later on in a child's life it is often based around what the child cannot do rather than what they can do. This is not in line with the view of the EYFS (DCSF, 2008) that all children are unique and have different ways of learning, nor the ethos of the National Portage Association as discussed in Chapter 3, which encourages families to always celebrate what the child can do.

Parents have also suggested that the process of diagnosis can have a devastating impact on them. It may well encourage them to question whether or not they are capable of bringing up a child with SEND. Parents may see the future as dark and negative, and they may well turn to books or the internet for information about the child's disability (Hodge, 2005). The internet in particular has brought with it many advances, but one of the negative aspects of it is that parents may rely on it too much. Sometimes information on the internet is not reliable and does not always give a balanced view on certain diagnoses. Parents can fail to see their child as an individual with unique gifts, talents and abilities which should be celebrated. Caroline White (2017) wrote about her experiences of having a child with Down syndrome and her seeming insatiability for books that discussed this condition. Looking back on the situation 20 years later, she realises that rather than enjoying the early years of her child's life, she ended up focusing on them with too much of a clinical perspective. Parents have also commented that the 'label becomes more significant than the nature of the child' (Hodge, 2005: 2). This seems sad to me, and suggests that gaining 'a label' is not always the benefit that some may think it is.

REFLECTION

- Have you ever considered the effect of a diagnosis on parents of a child with SEND before?

- In what way do you think that you could support them through or after a diagnosis?

- What are your views on focusing too much on what a child cannot do rather than what they can do?

THE BENEFITS OF THE LABELLING OF A SEND

It can:

- Support parents in gaining information about the child.
- Offer information relating to financial support and other services which support the child and family.
- Bring with it a sense of relief. The parents who talked to me about their child who was not diagnosed until their teenage years felt relief. Their child is one of a handful of children affected in the UK and they were put in touch with charities in the USA. They found this to be very enlightening and it helped them to realise why their child displayed some of the behaviours that she did.
- Support the family to either start or continue the rather stressful assessment processes discussed in Chapter 4 – this is when the effectiveness of observations and paperwork completed with the parents and child are so important.
- Sustain the school and other agencies involved with the family to develop Education, Health and Care Plans for children which will support them through their time in education and also bring together the multi-agency support for the child (DFE and DOH, 2014).
- Encourage professionals to put together plans, which should be written with parents and which will support the child's education and how it is delivered. These documents should also encourage the 'can do' approach to learning and take note of any individual ways the child learns best.

- Encourage professionals and clinicians to draw on information related to a particular disability to support the child. However, this can also encourage the 'homogenizing' that MacNaughton discusses as it can encourage all children with a certain SEND to be brought together rather than focusing on each child's individuality (McNaughton et al. 2004).

PERSONAL NOTE 6.1

Early on in my career I started working with a young boy with Down syndrome. This condition was new to me, and when I told people of my slight apprehension they said to me 'oh it will be fine – children with Down syndrome are loving, happy and always laughing'. The child did have these characteristics, but he was also fiercely independent, stubborn and at times deeply troubled.

Initially I found supporting this child very challenging as his independent nature also meant that he would often become cross and angry and could be aggressive to both children and adults. However, as I continued to work alongside him I started to notice when the anger was appearing and so could distract him with another activity that he enjoyed more. It taught me that each child is unique and will always have their own individual traits and idiosyncrasies and ways of doing things.

A label can support other children in the setting to recognise that the child is different and may help them to understand the child's difficulties and they way that they behave (mentalhelp.net).

THE CHALLENGES OF LABELLING A CHILD

- It can cause the child as they grow to suffer low self-esteem and therefore create social and emotional issues in later life. This can be really difficult for the child concerned and their family.
- Teachers and practitioners working with the child may have lower expectations of what the child can do – this can therefore set the child up to fail if their achievements are not celebrated.
- Peers can be particularly unkind to children with disabilities. The child may be bullied and therefore feel very vulnerable. Sophie in case study 6.1 always goes through feelings of anxiety during transitions – particularly at the end of the school year when children she likes and has built friendships with go into different classes. This also brings anxiety to her mother, Joanne, as she seeks to support her through this process.
- Other issues with a child can be masked. Non-English-speaking children who may speak English as an additional language might have other issues apart from their communication needs. This can be difficult, particularly if the parents are struggling to come to terms with a child's disability. Parents from other cultures can see disability very differently. This can be because of cultural issues or maybe because of a lack of understanding of particular disabilities (Borkett, 2018).

In 2019 at a music festival I attended, the poet John Osbourne spoke these words – 'just because something is diagnosed doesn't mean that it is the end'. Such a true statement, and one that parents and practitioners alike should hold on to.

REFLECTION

- In what ways do you think diagnosis and the labelling process can support children?
- Do you think it is a positive or a negative procedure?
- Have you had any experience of this, and if so, how did you react?

DEALING WITH THE GRIEF OF PARENTS AND FAMILY MEMBERS AFTER A DIAGNOSIS

You may never have considered this aspect of disability before, but parents have discussed with me in the past how when they receive a diagnosis of a SEND they can go through a period of grieving. Glass (2000) discusses the experience of Holly's parents when their much wanted daughter received a diagnosis of Down syndrome five days after birth. This happened before there were amniocentesis tests available and the parents had no idea that there was anything amiss with their child. Glass discusses the seeming brutality of medical staff who told her that Holly may never walk, talk, have friends or be able to learn. Her parents were, as expected, horrified – however, they already loved her and wanted to give her opportunities to do the same as any other child. In the book, Glass describes a relationship that Holly's mother fostered with a nurse in hospital who listened to Holly's parents, answered questions and went and found information relating to Down syndrome. She painted a much brighter picture of Holly's life, whilst taking time to sit with Holly's parents sensitively supporting them through this difficult time. She gave them time, space and empathy whilst they went through this period of grieving for the child that they had not had.

This concept of grief is something that parents go through quite often, and it can happen either at birth or later on in a child's life when a diagnosis of a SEND is made. Parents of children who are later diagnosed with autism talk about the knowing that something was not quite right with their child's development. With autism, diagnosis can take much longer. Autism is a disability that affects a child's communication, cognitive and developmental skills. Therefore three professionals need to observe the child. These would be a speech and language therapist, a paediatrician and an educational psychologist. When these observations have been completed, the diagnosis can be made. As we saw in Sophie's case, this may not be until the child is already in education.

Parents describe the 'ambiguous loss and chronic sorrow' (2007: 4) of receiving a diagnosis and an ending of parental expectations and hopes for the 'ideal' child that they gave birth to. Lowes and Lyne (2000) liken the time of waiting for a diagnosis to the bereavement period after the death of somebody. Gregory (2019) describes the five stages of grief according to Kübler-Ross as follows:

1. Denial and isolation – not wanting to accept the diagnosis and the need to isolate yourself from everyone. This may particularly affect the parents of a child with SEND who might prefer to distance themselves from other children with a similar diagnosis.
2. Anger – the feeling of why me? Was it my fault? Why would something like this happen to me/us? What could I have done to prevent this?
3. Bargaining – thinking that if only I had done something differently this may not have happened. If only I had played more with my child in their early years. If only I had talked to my child more this might have been prevented.
4. Depression – parents can become depressed after the diagnosis has been made. It is imperative during this time that parents are supported by practitioners who can 'be there'. This may be to give support, to show empathy to the parents and to maybe signpost them to other services that can support them.
5. Acceptance – finally parents can accept their child's needs and they are ready to support them as they grow.

So practitioners may think that once a diagnosis has been made and parents have gone through these stages, all will be well; however Lowes and Lyne (2001) suggest that these stages of grief continue as the child grows. They suggest that each time the child goes through a 'rite of passage' the grief can return and parents go back in their mind to the diagnosis and the acceptance that their child is different in some way. During these times practitioners need to be there for parents even if they can be difficult to engage with. They may seem aloof, they may not want to be with people, but it is vital that practitioners do not give up that support. Maybe a text or a phone call just to check up on the parent is all that is needed.

REFLECTION

- Have you ever considered that parents of children with SEND can experience feelings of grief?
- Why do you think this might be?
- What could you do to support them?

CASE STUDY 6.2

Grace

Grace was two years old and had been diagnosed with global developmental delay. She was the much-loved and longed-for child of Wendy and George. Grace had been receiving Portage support in the home for around nine months since the health visitor had picked up that there were some difficulties with her development. Wendy and George were not particularly keen to receive Portage as they felt that Grace would catch up and they could not imagine that there was anything wrong with her development.

After six months of support from the Portage team it was recommended that Grace start to attend a specialist playgroup for children with SEND. Wendy was not keen on this and was quick to point out that she would not be leaving her alone at the playgroup. So Wendy and Grace began to attend. Initially Grace spent much of her time alongside Wendy, but as the months went on Grace became more independent and would happily play alongside the other children. Six months went by and Wendy still felt the need to stay with Grace.

After nine months of them attending I suggested that maybe Wendy should leave Grace. The only way that Wendy would agree to this was if she sat upstairs where there was a room where the children playing in the playgroup below could be watched. This was agreed to and, although initially Grace would cry when her Mum left her, she soon was happy to be left alone. After another three months I spoke again to Wendy and suggested that maybe she could leave Grace and go to the shops whilst she was playing. Wendy was not happy but started leaving her for half an hour each session. Slowly this period of time was extended until Wendy would happily leave Grace for the entire session.

Consider

- Who was it that needed the support most in this case study, Grace or Wendy?
- Why do you think she persisted with staying with Grace for so long?
- How would you support a parent in a similar situation?

The final section of this chapter will focus on the *whole* family and the impact a child with SEND can have on the entire family.

RELATIONSHIPS WITHIN THE FAMILY WHEN A CHILD HAS SEND

WHAT IS A FAMILY?

Families come in different types and have changed greatly over the past 50 years. Recently there have been many studies carried out in order to attempt to define the role of the family, particularly in the West (Flandrin, 1979; Stone, 1977). However all of these studies have looked particularly at families living in this part of the world and not at families across the world. However, Chambers (2012) suggests that recent changes to family structures and a growth in women's employment have had an impact on the role of families and the need for early childcare.

The idea of the nuclear family as espoused by Parsons (1971), where a family is made up of a mother, father and two children, has changed greatly in the 21st century. Now it is not unusual to have families where parents of the same gender are bringing up children, single parents may make the decision to raise a child alone or grandparents may be raising children for some reason, as well as blended families where parents may have new partners and so children from different partnerships live together. Whether or not you agree with these types of family, it is vital that practitioners do not discriminate against the different forms of family and that they offer them the support they require (Borkett, 2018).

Lindon (2012), in the context of working with children from other cultures who have children with SEND, accentuates the need for practitioners to discover in a sensitive way some of the practices and firmly held beliefs of families which might 'spill over' to the way they live. Having had experience of working with families from across the globe, I have often been surprised by the different cultural views of disability. For many families from developing cultures sons are seen as more important than daughters. Therefore if a family has a daughter who also has special needs they can be forgotten and their needs taken less seriously. In other parts of the world such as Africa, children born with special needs can be abandoned at birth and left to die outside. Although this would be unheard of in the UK this does still go on in some parts of the world. Therefore we cannot assume that families coming to the UK to settle who may have children with SEND will take their disabilities as seriously as they should (Borkett, 2018).

THE IMPACT OF DISABILITY ON THE FAMILY
GRANDPARENTS

Having a child with a disability can have a major impact on all of the family. Over the past 20 or 30 years there has been an increase in the number of grandparents looking after grandchildren whilst their parents work. Research by the University of Oxford (n.d.) makes the case that grandparents' contributions to the care of their grandchildren can have a positive effect on children's wellbeing. However, Mitchell (2008) suggests that more research is needed to find out the effect on grandparents when their grandchildren have SEND. She does however make the case that the parents of children with SEND experience more stress finding suitable childcare, and that grandparents can offer emotional support to parents who may be feeling very vulnerable. In the case study relating to Sophie, her grandparents had struggled to accept the fact that she had a SEND. They felt that she was a little bit slow but would 'catch up eventually'. This caused added stress for Joanne, who wanted them to realise that this was not the case and to accept

Sophie as the child that she was. When the diagnosis was given, Joanne became very concerned about the impact it may have on Sophie's grandparents, but when she did share the news the grandparents took it on board without question.

SIBLINGS

Undeniably the siblings of children with SEND can be affected by their brother's or sister's disability; however, there has been little research carried out in relation to this. As I prepared to write this chapter I looked in the indexes of 10 books relating to SEND and none of them mentioned the impact on siblings. Dunn suggests that:

> the role of siblings as peers is rarely given more than passing mention and the complexities of relationships and affectional bonds between siblings themselves, and with parents, are traditionally underestimated and neglected. (2000: 97)

Milevsky (2014) suggests that siblings play a vital part in the life of children with SEND. The University of Michigan (2009) also notes that the siblings of children with SEND often learn different and complementary skills that are related to caring. They suggest that siblings learn how to be patient, show kindness and empathy, have a greater acceptance of difference and diversity, and gain greater insight into how people develop. Dunn (2000), who carried out a small piece of research relating to the perspectives of non-disabled children on their disabled siblings, found similar outcomes. Both discovered that siblings can learn a lot from having a brother/sister with a disability. However, both make the case that for some siblings life can become quite negative. They may suffer emotional stress if they are worried about their siblings, particularly if they have a degenerative condition that is life limiting. They might also feel ignored as their parents are more involved with the care of the child with SEND. They may feel that they miss out on outings or holidays if these are difficult for a child who may need aids and for whom moving away from the home can become stressful. It is important to note here that all siblings go through some kind of rivalry, but that this can be exacerbated if one sibling has SEND and may be able to get away with more than another.

Milevsky (2014) also suggests that siblings may have questions about their brother/sister's disabilities that they are afraid to ask their parents. This might be because they do not know how to ask the questions or that they are afraid of what the answer might be. He goes on to stress the importance of parents being open and honest about the children with SEND. Dunn (2000) agrees, stating that it is important for parents to share the perspective of the child with their siblings.

As mentioned above, Dunn (2000) carried out a small piece of research relating to the perspectives of non-disabled children on their disabled siblings. She, like the University of Michigan, discovered that often siblings can learn a lot from having a brother/sister with SEND and that the effects can be both positive and negative. Dunn (2000) agrees that siblings can sometimes be left out and their needs not considered when the main focus of the parents is on the child with SEND. She also suggests that there can be differences in the amount of affection and attention that the sibling gains from their parents. However, on a positive note she believes that siblings can become their brother/sister's greatest advocates. Recognising that they may find it easier to interpret their sibling's communication, behaviours and emotions, she discovered that often children have as much knowledge about their sibling's disabilities and can explain things to adults as well as the parents because they are slightly removed from the role of the parent. Dunn also makes the case that siblings can create strategies for communicating with their brothers or sisters, which helps to build a positive relationship whereby all children in the family are heard.

REFLECTION

- Have you ever thought about the effects of having a brother/sister with a SEND before?
- How could you support a sibling who has a brother/sister with SEND?
- What challenges do you think they may face?

Through this chapter you will have:

- considered the historical concept of the practitioner role when working alongside families when children have special educational needs and disabilities (SEND)
- understood how parents may relate to the diagnosis and 'label' of a particular SEND/medical condition and whether this can affect the parents' relationship with the child
- considered relationships within the family, particularly in relation to the siblings of children with SEND.

END OF CHAPTER QUESTIONS

- Over the past 50 years the role of the parent in a child's education has become far more complex – what are the benefits and challenges of this?
- How might you support a parent who is struggling with the grief of finding out that their child has a disability?
- How might you support the younger siblings of a child with Down syndrome?

FURTHER READING

Borkett, P.A. (2018) Working with families. In: *Cultural Diversity and Inclusion in Early Years Education*. Abingdon: Routledge.

This particular chapter focuses on the importance of working with families who come from the developing world and who may view SEND very differently from those families who come from the West.

Coffey, C. (2013) The pros and cons of labelling a chid with a developmental delay. www.thejournal.ie/readme/column-the-pros-and-cons-of-labelling-a-child-with-developmental-delay

This paper discusses some of the benefits and challenges that parents go through when their child undergoes the diagnostic process of getting a SEND. It discusses how this process can affect the parents emotionally, but also the benefits that can come in terms of financial and family support.

White, C. (2017) *The Label – A Story for Families*. Brighton: MENCAP.

This very short book is a simply written autobiographical account of the journey a parent went through when her first child was born with Down syndrome. It tells of how she tried to seek advice from the internet and books but then eventually fell in love with her child and learnt to love them for who they were.

7

EDUCATIONAL PROVISION FOR CHILDREN WITH SPECIAL EDUCATIONAL NEEDS AND DISABILITY

The previous chapter discussed the importance of forging strong partnerships with families and carers. This is vitally important when parents are seeking educational provision for their children, and so this chapter will discuss and examine the provisions available for children with SEND.

By the end of this chapter you will have:

- understood some of the political background of educational provision for children with SEND
- examined how mainstream schools can support children with SEND
- reflected on the inclusive nature of special schools.

O nce more I have tried to ensure this chapter is up to date by visiting different settings here in the UK. I have had the opportunity to speak to practitioners and to discover what aspects of their provision they feel are particularly important to children with SEND. They also comment on some of the benefits and challenges of inclusive education and educating children with special educational needs and disabilities.

Previous chapters have introduced the reader to some of the legislation and policy relating to children with SEND (Chapter 1). This chapter begins with information concerning the medical and social models of disability. Whilst this was touched on in Chapter 1, it needs more exploration in this chapter as it sets the foundation for education as it is in the 21st century.

The chapter then goes on to discuss education and the choices that parents have when considering where they want their children to be educated. Discussion will then focus on how mainstream schools support children with SEND. It will consider the benefits and challenges of inclusive education and will also explore how the political landscape can affect this provision.

The final section of the chapter will focus on the inclusivity of special schools. Sometimes special schools get a bad press. In the introduction I discussed my own ongoing personal dilemma in terms of inclusion and the place of special schools in education. I firmly believe that in the UK children with disabilities should be able to experience inclusion in early years settings, particularly as the curriculum relates to 'the unique child' and has at its centre the importance of play and learning through exploration. However, as children become older they may need a different provision that is better suited with smaller classes and different curricula and which incorporates medical programmes such as speech and language therapy, physio and occupational therapy, support from a dietitian and on-site medical care. Because of the children's particular needs, special schools have to offer a bespoke package of education and care to children in their schools – this to my mind comes under the umbrella of inclusion.

THE MEDICAL AND SOCIAL MODELS OF DISABILITY

These models were introduced in Chapter 1, along with the evolving role of education through history was discussed. However, much of educational provision for children with SEND relates to these models so it is important that they should be discussed in a little more detail here. Allan (2010: 604) suggests that the 'sociology of disability' was first introduced in the 1980s when people were beginning to realise that special education was not the panacea that people had first thought. Institutional structures and practices were beginning to emerge and those interested in the education of children with SEND were becoming concerned about some of the 'structural and attitudinal barriers' that were emerging from special education (p.604).

THE MEDICAL MODEL OF DISABILITY

In the late 19th and early 20th centuries the diagnosis of special needs was, in the main, something carried out by medical staff. This therefore meant that disability became a medicalised issue. Words such as prevention, treatment, clinical and cure were used and children were considered to have a handicap and therefore to be unable to do things for themselves, make decisions or to live alongside their peers. At this time the concept that children had a voice was never considered. Children with a disability were thought of as being second rate to their peers and certainly not 'normal'. The medical model also suggests that people were 'disabled by their impairments or differences' (disabilitynottinghamshire, n.d.) and focuses on what the child cannot do rather than what they can do. This is also known as the deficit model of education (Education-Line, 2008), which views the child as being vulnerable and weak.

An example of the medical model might be a child with cerebral palsy who has difficulties with their physical skills but is very able cognitively. In the 1990s a child like this would probably have been put into a special school because of their physical needs, but their cognitive abilities would have been completely overlooked. This may mean that the child would lose their cognitive skills because they were not being nurtured or even recognised.

CASE STUDY 7.1 —————————————

Sunil

Sunil was eight years old and was blind. He grew up in the 1990s when children who were blind were often educated in special schools. He attended a school for visually impaired children in London, which his parents had chosen because it was smaller and had classes with a higher ratio of adults and less children than in mainstream education. The school was also set up for children to learn Braille but still followed the National Curriculum, which ensured that Sunil, who was very bright, would learn the same things that his older brother did in mainstream education.

At times Sunil became quite frustrated by other children in the class whose cognitive needs were more impaired that his own. He would often hit or bite the other children, particularly if he was bored because the level of the work was too easy for him. It was decided that for some of the time Sunil should attend the local mainstream primary school which was nearby. Staff from the special school initially visited the primary school and talked to staff about some of the adaptations Sunil would need. This included the placing of furniture and resources, and a couple of children were chosen to befriend Sunil and sit with him during his time in the school. He went for a number of visits, and any issues that emerged were sorted quickly. Initially Sunil visited once a week, but the visits became so successful that this was quickly increased to three times a week. Both staff teams were responsible for providing Sunil with the resources that he needed when he attended the primary school. A teaching assistant would also accompany Sunil, more because of health and safety than anything else.

(Continued)

As time went on staff at the special school saw real changes in Sunil's emotional wellbeing. He no longer became frustrated in school and really enjoyed the relationships he made at the primary school. It was then decided that he should move to the primary school for half a week and spend the other half at the special school. Sunil coped with this well and continued to grow in confidence and ability.

This experience was not only beneficial to Sunil but it began a pattern of working that continues to this day. If children in the special school are able to cope with mainstream school they will often spend a couple of sessions in the school too. The children in the primary school benefit as they can understand difference and diversity in a very positive way.

Consider

- Have you ever thought about how split placements for children can be beneficial?
- What might the benefits and challenges be of a split provision?
- How different might Sunil's educational experience be in 2020?

THE SOCIAL MODEL OF DISABILITY

The social model of disability began to emerge around the time of the United Nations Convention on the Rights of the Child (1989) and the Salamanca Statement (UNESCO, 1994), both of which were discussed in Chapter 1. They are based on a human rights model and believe that it is society that causes children with SEND to fail or to not achieve. As we read in Chapter 1, around this time, Warnock (1978 [2005]) was reviewing education for children with SEND and in agreement with the social model of disability believed that, in the main, children with SEND should wherever possible be educated in their community primary schools. The social model also recognises that all should have a voice and that those with disabilities should have a voice in their own lives. If children are non-verbal they should have access to augmentative communication aids, which in turn will give them a voice.

Oliver (quoted in Allan and Slee, 2008) made the suggestion that sometimes the social model is considered by some as an idea or a concept when maybe it should be a principle that is a fundamental truth that has the capacity to make changes to the lives of those with disabilities, both nationally and internationally.

When the new Code of Practice was introduced in 2014 there was a real shift from the old Code, which had been written from a medical perspective, to the newer Code, which rightly focuses far more on the social model, human rights and parents' and children's views and opinions (DFE and DOH, 2014).

EDUCATIONAL PROVISION IN THE UK

The importance of educational provision is set out in the SEND Code of Practice (DFE and DOH, 2014). This gives parents and their children the opportunity to choose which type of provision they attend. The Equality Act 2010 makes the case that settings need to make 'reasonable adjustment' to meet the needs of children with SEND, yet there is no real clarification as to what those adjustments should be (Borkett, 2012). The Code also introduces the local offer, which was discussed in Chapter 4 – this charges local authorities to ensure that parents are made aware of what school provision is available for children with SEND.

As has been considered previously, all early years settings need to follow the Early Years Foundation Stage (DCSF, 2008), which sets out that all children are unique. This focuses not only on the different interests and fascinations of young children but also on their specific ways of learning. These differing needs will very much relate to a child's abilities, culture and fascinations. This is something that practitioners need to consider when planning for children with SEND as they may have different requirements in terms of communication, interests and their ways of learning.

PERSONAL NOTE 7.1

Equal opportunities

When I was lecturing I often encouraged students to think about equal opportunities and what this really meant. Students would often say that equal opportunities are about ensuring that all children receive the same provision. When questioning their responses I would suggest that different resources may be needed for a child who was visually impaired to that of a seeing child. They started to realise that equal opportunities is more about ensuring that every child is given the opportunity and the resources to explore, develop and learn in the way that they need. This is very different from giving children all the same opportunities.

Consider

- What does the term equal opportunities mean to you?
- How do you ensure that children receive equal opportunities?
- What are the challenges of equal opportunities?

Children with SEND need an educational provision that, as with all children, is tailored to them. However, their requirements may be greater and might relate to other services such as speech and language, physio and occupational therapy. Some children may already have an Education, Health Care Plan (EHCP) in place. This sets out their needs and requirements and enables settings to write targets which are clearly linked to the plan and to other treatments which they receive from multi-agency teams. Others may not be at this stage as they may not yet have a diagnosis of a SEND, but their needs are as important. Because of the geographical location of one of the settings that I visited, children do not get an EHCP until they go into school. This is because the local authority views itself as being completely inclusive so does not feel it is necessary until children start school. Whilst this would seem to be a positive thing, practitioners in the setting felt that it meant that children entering the setting with SEND were sometimes hampered by this decision. It meant that information was not necessarily shared with key workers, who needed to put targets in place to establish with the children.

Often, inclusive provisions come at a higher cost to the local authority as there may be particular resources and equipment that children need. These may be required in both mainstream and special schools, but in mainstream schools particularly, staff may need to be trained in using the equipment. This will, in the main, be the responsibility of the local authority to provide these, but at what cost?

Whilst I was visiting a special school the teacher stated that some children enter the school at five after they have been in a mainstream nursery, and others come in at years 1 or 2, having again previously been in mainstream provision but struggled there. This may suggest as the DFES did in 2001 that 'mainstream education may not be right at particular stages of education', and agrees with Shehata (2016), who points out that children can begin to struggle if their cognitive functioning diminishes over time.

However, the choice of educational provision for children is nearly always the responsibility of parents and carers (Smith et al., 2018), as stated in both Codes of Practice, and it is important to note here that schools do have a responsibility to accommodate children with SEND if required. However, Ofsted has found that some teachers continue to 'make insufficient adaptations to mainstream curriculum' (2004: 174) to ensure that children with SEND make progress.

Research carried out into the role of teaching assistants, who are often employed to work with children with SEND, discovered that children could become too dependent on them if they were permanently attached to particular children (Hazell, 2017). The revised Code of Practice (DFE and DOH, 2014) makes the case that whilst teaching assistants are important to the education of children and that they are very much part of the teaching team, the final responsibility for a child's development and learning rests with the teacher.

REFLECTION

- How important do you think the role of the teaching assistant is in children's education?

- What do you think are the benefits and challenges of the role?

- How might teachers work with teaching assistants to ensure that the teacher is kept up to date with the needs of the child?

In Chapter 4 the difficult circumstances that England's current SEND provision are experiencing were mentioned, and it would seem pertinent to discuss this in more detail here as currently it is having a huge impact on high numbers of children. Recently a review of SEND was conducted by the Education Select Committee (Parliament UK, 2019a). This committee is charged with ensuring that administration, policy and expenditure are being used wisely and that policies are being properly implemented. The Committee discovered that many of the changes that should have been set out in line with the SEND Code of Practice (2014) have not been executed and that the changes have been hampered by 'poor administration'. Alongside this the country has been in a period of austerity, which means that local authority budgets have been cut back enormously, which in turn has had an impact on whether they have been able to implement the 'local offer' as effectively as it should have been.

This has also had a negative effect on the resourcing of all schools but particularly those that meet the needs of children with SEND, which may need expensive equipment and high staffing levels. It has had a further impact on the continuing professional development (CPD) that teachers and teaching assistants receive. One practitioner told me recently that the only training offered at the moment through local authorities is safeguarding because this is legislative. Within the documentation gathered by the Select Committee it was detailed that out of the £140 million assigned to SEND education, only £1.5 – 2.3 million is spent on training. It is hard to see how practitioners can effectively work with children with SEND if they are unable to access appropriate training.

The review also concluded that parents should not be expected to 'know the system', but should be offered support to understand what their rights are in terms of their child's education and be supported in making the decisions of which provision best meets their child's needs. Finally, it suggests that parents are being left 'exhausted' by a system that is not yet efficient enough to support children and their families. So we see that currently SEND provision is in crisis.

REFLECTION

- How can these current difficulties with SEND provision affect young children?
- How can these current difficulties with SEND provision affect parents?
- How can these current difficulties with SEND provision affect practitioners?

THE BENEFITS OF MAINSTREAM EDUCATION FOR CHILDREN WITH SEND

Mainstream inclusive education follows the ethos of the social model of disability and puts the onus on schools to ensure that all children should be able to attend their local community school. However, schools must be prepared to open their doors to children with SEND as it is not just a case of giving them access to a particular location (DFES, 2001); it also means that the ethos of the school has to be inclusive and that practitioners care about all children and want the best from them. In 2004 the Labour government produced a paper entitled 'Removing the Barriers to Achievement'; this launched its strategy for SEND (DFES, 2004). Hornby (2015) suggests that more recently views on mainstream education for children with SEND have changed, and that inclusion is becoming difficult to achieve in practice. This may be due to the differing priorities of the government. In 2001 the government was keen that children with SEND should be educated in mainstream schools. If we move to the present, as discussed in the previous section, we see a system in crisis, which might suggest that the Conservative government have taken their eye off the ball in terms of inclusion.

MAINSTREAM EDUCATION - A PARENTAL CHOICE?

Many parents prefer to send their children to a mainstream school because they want them to be educated alongside their peers. They may have been to pre-school groups in their community and parents feel that it is important that friendships made there should be continued into the next phase of education. Runswick-Cole (2008) carried out research into parental views on education, discovering that parents choose mainstream school for a variety of different reasons. Some believe the following:

- If children go to a mainstream school they are less likely to pick up unwanted behaviour than if they are in special education. One parent's son (in the study) had autism, and copying behaviours are a common trait of those with this disorder (National Autistic Society, 2016a).
- If children were in mainstream schools they would witness appropriate behaviours being used in social situations and would hopefully copy these, thus meaning that they are better able to socialise with their peers (Gupta et al., 2014).
- It is better for children to be educated in mainstream as it was felt that this better replicated society.
- A child's emotional wellbeing may be improved if they are educated in mainstream and they will be better able to develop 'social competence', which Guralnick describes as being 'the ability of young children to successfully and appropriately select and carry out their interpersonal goals' (1989: 276). This in turn can affect a child's independence skills.

It is also vital that children with SEND in mainstream provision have access to the same kind of resources in terms of the curriculum and access to equipment (Runswick-Cole, 2008). This can enable their independence to grow and allow them to experience important life skills such as:

- toileting
- sharing
- listening
- communication.

These skills may be more likely to be picked up in a mainstream school where children are taught alongside their peers, rather than in special education. Opportunities for children to interact with higher functioning peers in mainstream is also a great advantage and can have a positive affect on children's play and learning (Gupta et al., 2014). So too can children's communication and interactive skills improve when they are in mainstream education.

REFLECTION

- How do you view the education of children with SEND?

- Do you believe that mainstream schools should be inclusive of all children?

- What do you see as being some of the challenges of mainstream education for children with SEND?

WHAT DO SETTINGS NEED TO DO TO ENSURE THAT THEY ARE INCLUSIVE TO ALL?

Having established that mainstream provision should be an entitlement for all, what is it that settings need to do to ensure that they are appropriate for all children? In Chapters 2 and 3 I focused on the importance of different communication systems to support children with SEND, and also the importance of the environment and how this can support/challenge children who can become overstimulated by bright colours. A vital aspect of ensuring inclusive practice is to make certain that the ethos of the setting is agreed by all. It cannot and should not be just the SENCO's responsibility to make the setting inclusive – everyone needs to be on board. This can mean, as suggested in Chapter 2, that practitioners need to be challenged to consider their own views of inclusion as a top priority before anything else. Case study 7.2 illustrates this point.

CASE STUDY 7.2

All children need is a cuddle?

I was working in a setting in the East Midlands as a SENCO. The setting was about to establish a nursery and so it was my job to write the policies relating to SEND, train practitioners in inclusive processes and ensure that the practice in the setting was positive and relevant to all. I therefore decided to bring a colleague on board who was a Portage worker in the setting. Right at the start of the training we decided to focus on the ethos that the nursery would sign up to – we felt it was important that those working there should establish how they would be inclusive to all.

Immediately we stumbled upon issues. Practitioners were uncertain as to how to support children with physical difficulties who might need support when moving around. Others were unsure that the cultural needs of children could be met in such a setting. Other practitioners believed that it was better for children with speech and language difficulties to be educated in special provision where therapists could support their communication more intensely. To say that I was disheartened at the end of this meeting was an understatement. However, I went away and reflected on this and the next meeting was held in the space that the nursery would use. Collectively we discussed what could be done to support children's physical needs, ensuring that there was lots of space around furniture for children to move. The more we talked about the issues, the more confident staff seemed to be that things would be ok.

The third meeting discussed the cultural issues that might arise whilst trying to ensure the setting was inclusive. Many different languages were spoken in the community and people had different cultural practices/traditions. Many parents had quite differing views on disability. However, because of this multicultural milieu some of the staff members came from these different cultures. They were able to explain the background to some of the public's views on SEND. As practitioners began to understand this they too seemed more confident to embrace inclusivity for all.

During the last session the setting's speech and language therapist came to talk to the practitioners. She spoke about the need for all children to communicate with one another and also introduced Makaton signing to the practitioners. She briefly discussed how the environment could be made language-rich with pictures, signs and photographs. And so the setting opened its doors.

My role was to regularly go into the setting and observe practice. After a couple of visits I came upon an issue – in the baby room a member of staff always seemed to be cuddling a child with Down syndrome. The child was able to crawl around and enjoyed playing with the other children in the group. I decided to talk to the member of staff and see why she was acting in this way. I discovered that she really did not understand the needs of the child and so thought it was safer to cuddle her rather than to let her engage with the other children in case she got hurt. I decided that she needed some mentoring and so she came out with myself and the other Portage worker and saw how we worked with the children and families. Gradually things started to change; she became more confident in playing with the children and encouraging them to try new things.

Consider

- Have you ever found yourself in this kind of situation? If so, how did you deal with it?
- Can you understand the needs of the practitioner?
- What more could the SENCO do to support practitioners in the setting?

STAFF TRAINING

It is vital that practitioners are trained appropriately when supporting all children, but especially those who have SEND. Children may have medical issues whereby staff are required to put in place interventions which can be obtrusive and difficult to administer. In 2015 the DFE wrote:

> A child's mental and physical health should be properly supported in school, so that the pupil can play a full and active role in school life, remain healthy and achieve their academic potential. (DFE, 2015)

I talked with practitioners about their training needs recently as a result of news in the media discussed earlier that suggested that CPD was non-existent. As is frequently the case, private and voluntary settings have to fund their own training if it is deemed necessary. One manager who owns three nurseries in the north of the country told me that she sees training around SEND and medical issues as being vital to all staff. When I asked who the settings' SENCOs were, I was told that the nursery manager oversees this and then cascades some training to the key workers of the particular children. However, when it came to medical needs the key workers would receive training first hand.

This group of settings have always tried to ensure that they are inclusive to all and have had many children with SEND through their doors over the past 25 years. However, with the growing medical and cognitive needs of children with SEND, particularly those who have been born prematurely, they find it harder to be inclusive because the medical, physical and cognitive needs of children can be so immense that they feel they cannot meet those needs adequately. Blackburn warns that there needs to be greater training for practitioners working with children who have been born prematurely and may therefore have a whole host of difficulties to deal with. She descibes the dilemma regarding training for practitioners working in education:

> Teachers and educational psychologists receive little formal training about preterm birth and are often not aware of appropriate strategies to support preterm children in the classroom. Informing teachers about the special constellation of problems following preterm birth is crucial in preparing them to support the growing number of children entering schools in the coming years. (Blackburn, n.d.: 1)

A PLAY-BASED PEDAGOGY

One of the reasons why I believe that inclusion in mainstream early years settings is possible is because of the play-based pedagogy advocated throughout the EYFS. During my visit to a setting recently I witnessed a new way of working with children, called the Curiosity Approach. This particular setting has a long history of engaging with heuristic play, which promotes the use of natural objects that encourage children to use their innate curiosity to explore, feel and experience natural materials and to make up their own play with these. It places less focus on plastic toys that may hamper children's play (Community Playthings, n.d.). The Curiosity Approach is similar in terms of natural components but it also uses 'authentic resources', whether they are recycled or made up of loose parts (Hellyn and Bennett, 2017). They may be natural resources such as conkers, acorns, or pines cones. They may also be artefacts or old household objects such as cups and saucers, glasses. They may also include used tea leaves from used tea bags. On the day that I visited, the rooms still had areas that you would expect from a nursery, but rather than them having plastic cups and saucers they had earthenware ones. Children were playing with glass bottles in the water tray. The tea leaves from flavoured tea bags were in a 'tuff spot' and all the children were engaged in the play – discussing what the tea smelt like and what they could do with it, and were carefully spooning it into different textured pots. Hannaby (2019) writes that since orchestrating this approach children seem to be learning at a deeper level, their communication is more sustained and their discussions with their peers are more intense, relating to what the objects can do, how they feel, and what they are becoming. Parents also have noticed that children are more interested in natural objects and their play is more sustained at home.

Whilst I was at the setting I observed a young child with SEND playing. The child, who is just three and struggles visually, was playing in the water tray, pouring water from a container into narrow-topped glass bottles and squealing with delight as the water flowed over the top. She then moved to the home corner which, rather than having shop-bought cupboards, was formed of wooden bricks which partitioned off the area. Here she spent 20 minutes moving wooden food from one container to another, talking to a staff member about what she was doing. At singing time she happily joined a large group and sung and signed nursery songs. She was clearly engaged in her play and interested in those around her. Whilst it would be wrong of me to promote this kind of play over any others, it did seem to me to sustain all the children in the setting.

However, I do need to mention here that in trying to include children with SEND in mainstream schools this is seen by some as being detrimental to other children in the class. Mary Warnock, whose work has been discussed in previous chapters, changed her view about inclusion in 2005, stating that it had become a 'disastrous legacy'. Because of the rise in inclusive education in mainstream schools many special schools were closed down as there was not the demand for them; however, she felt that the government had gone too far in including all children and that those with autism, and those with behavioural and emotional issues really were not coping. She stated:

> Governments must come to recognise that even if inclusion is an ideal for society in general it may not always be an ideal for schools – it has gone too far and become a kind of mantra – it really is not working. (Warnock, 1978 [2005])

REFLECTION

- What are your views on the inclusion of children with SEND in mainstream provision?
- What do you see are the benefits for all children?
- What do you see are the challenges for all children?

THE BENEFITS OF ENHANCED RESOURCE UNITS

Enhanced resource units are often used to facilitate the needs of children with a particular disability on the site of a mainstream school. The school will usually focus the provision around a particular area of need such as visual or hearing impairments, communication difficulties or autism. The idea of these units is that children are educated in the mainstream school for much of the time and then they will go into the unit for more specific teaching. For instance, if the unit was for children with visual impairment then they may go there to learn Braille. For children with hearing impairment the unit may relate to the teaching of British Sign Language (BSL). For those children with communication difficulties the unit may give more specific teaching in listening and communication.

The numbers of pupils in these units are smaller, maybe eight to twelve in some or four to six in another, depending on the areas of need. There will always be a teacher and at least one teaching assistant in the class (DFE, 2015). Some of the benefits of these units are the increased staff ratio and low class numbers, and for some children that can make a significant difference to their learning. Other benefits are that children spend much of their time with their peers from the mainstream school, which aids their social and emotional development and supports the likelihood of building friendships. It also has an impact on the children in the main school who realise that not all children are the same and that some may need a little extra support. Tutt and Williams (2015: 44) suggest that these units provide a 'useful bridge' between mainstream and special provision. However, Hunt (2018) warns of a dilemma when placing children in a separate unit. He suggests that children in the unit may struggle with two different teams of teachers and teaching assistants and that staff may have differing expectations of the children. McCoy and Banks (2012), on the other hand, believe that units like these can be very effective in enhancing children's socialisation skills. Interestingly there has been little research carried out into the effectiveness of such units.

Having focused on the benefits of inclusive settings for children with SEND, the next section will focus on the inclusivity, benefits and challenges of special schools.

THE BENEFITS AND INCLUSIVITY OF SPECIAL SCHOOLS

Some readers may be looking at the title of this section and wondering if writing this book has affected my judgement, but as I set out in the introduction, I firmly believe in special schools. As I stated earlier in this chapter, many children with SEND need a bespoke education that not only focuses on their cognitive needs but also on their physical, medical and emotional needs. On a recent visit to a special school there were nine children in the year 1 class, one of whom had hearing and visual impairments and was not yet able to move around independently, neither did he have any verbal or augmentative communication skills. However, he did have the most wonderful smile and a gorgeous laugh when being communicated with. He was able to stand in a frame but had to be helped in and out by practitioners. Another child with Down syndrome was unable to move around and so spent much of her time in a wheelchair, except when practitioners were doing her twice-daily physiotherapy exercises. She was not yet able to communicate but had some comprehension of what was being said to her. In addition to these children there were four others in the class who were using Makaton to communicate. It would take a very exceptional mainstream school to be able to meet the needs of these children. However, it should also be noted that special schools are often criticised for following the medical model of disability, which separates children and focuses a lot more on their medical needs.

SPECIAL EDUCATION - A PARENTAL CHOICE?

Runswick-Cole (2008) discovered, when she researched the reasons why parents chose special schools for their children, that for one parent it was the chance for their child to start again. Years later she said that 'it had changed her child's life' and she was so pleased she had made this decision.

However, Connor (1997) argues that for some parents their choice of special provision is born out of their sense of loss at having a child with SEND, going on to suggest that parents believe that special schools offer greater protection to the child and shield parents from the daily reminder of mainstream that their child is different. This may seem quite a harsh view but it does go along with some of the views considered in Chapter 6.

Runswick-Cole (2008) suggests that for parents, special schools are sometimes seen as a 'safe haven' where staff will understand their child's needs, medical staff may be permanently on hand in an emergency and staff will be trained in different ways to work with children. She also records another parent who initially had their child educated in mainstream then had them moved quickly into special because they felt their child's needs were not being met. The parent believed that their child's needs were not being met. Other parents did, however, accept that although their children may start in mainstream, there may come a time when it would not be possible for them to remain there and so they may then need to go into special provision. I do feel that it is vital here to accept the fact that some parents feel that mainstream education is not right for their child and that special provision would be best. Parents know their children and I believe they should be supported by sensitive practitioners to make the decision that is right for them and their child.

HOW IS IT THAT SPECIAL SCHOOLS ARE INCLUSIVE?

In order to try and explain this I will draw on my own personal experience of working in special education during the 1990s. The school catered for children with severe learning difficulties from nursery up to age 18. During this time, within the local authority there were also separate primary and senior schools for those with moderate learning difficulties and then another for children with profound and multiple learning difficulties. However, with the increased number of children going into mainstream, as we saw in Warnock's work (2005), many special schools were closed. In this school I worked in the junior class. There were nine children, all with very differing needs, and three practitioners, one of whom was a teacher.

During the morning, activities would usually revolve around maths and English and would include time in the sensory room for some children. The children were required to follow the National Curriculum but many of them were achieving at the lower P levels, as explained in Chapter 4, so activities were mainly taught through play. The children also went swimming every week, had access to a specialist art therapist who taught them weekly, and every alternate week spent some time in the community. Sometimes this would be to a local café, or to a toy shop or to somewhere that linked with that term's topic. During the afternoons, focus moved to activities around other areas of the curriculum such as art and creativity, understanding of the world, and activities such as baking, planting and gardening, which fed into science. Here we see that although the children were separated from their peers, their education was varied and structured to ensure that the children learnt, albeit slightly differently.

Fifteen years later I became a governor in a special school that has some similarities to this school. The needs of the children here are very different and in some cases quite extreme. The majority of the children are in small classes with a mixture of needs being met. There is also one classroom where the needs of the children are so complex, and at times life limiting, that they require a much more specialist approach to development and learning through a range of sensory activities. Recently we have been discussing in meetings the needs of children who had been born prematurely and have a host of both medical and physical issues, trying to decide whether it is appropriate to separate these children from their peers and move them into a different class. The needs of these children puts a tremendous strain on practitioners, who have to carry out medical interventions such as inserting feeding tubes, giving children oxygen, as well as giving them much-needed physio and speech and language support. Although the practitioners are given appropriate training, it is a huge amount of responsibility for those who are paid at quite a low wage but whose responsibilities are immense. It was decided that the school should continue to educate the children in mixed classes but to ensure a slightly higher level of staffing to make certain all children receive the support they deserve. However, this of course has wider cost implications. So here we see a similar dilemma to that of inclusive classrooms in mainstream schools, where the needs of the children are so great that to include them all is a real challenge. There will be ongoing evaluation as to whether this was the correct choice but the governors felt it better to try and be inclusive by doing this.

REFLECTION

- Have you ever considered that special schools are inclusive environments for the education of children ?
- What do you think are the benefits of mixed ability groups?
- What do you think are the challenges of mixed ability groups?

THE BENEFITS OF SPECIAL SCHOOLS

There are many benefits of special schools. Some of these are:

- smaller classes with a higher staff:child ratio
- practitioners are trained in particular ways of working that support the children
- augmentative communication systems are embraced
- therapists and medical staff may work on site, ensuring that children do not have to travel weekly or fortnightly to appointments at the hospital
- each child will receive a bespoke education plan linked to their EHCP which will relate to their holistic needs – these plans will accommodate their cognitive needs as well as any medical plans from a range of medical professionals
- a different curriculum can be used for children that better suits their educational needs.

The following case study demonstrates how one particular child really blossomed when she went into a special school.

CASE STUDY 7.3

Rachel

Rachel was five years old and had recently been diagnosed with autism. She was the elder of two girls who got on very well together at home. Rachel had attended a mainstream nursery but had struggled with certain aspects of it. As with many children on the autistic spectrum she didn't like lots of noise and also became confused when activities changed. She would often run and hide in a corner when it was time to tidy up, get ready for dinner or go home. Singing and story time were a nightmare for Rachel because of the noise, so she would have her story and singing away from the other children. After much discussion between the nursery practitioners, her parents and professionals who supported Rebecca it was decided that she should go into a special primary school when she was five.

Initially Rachel found school quite hard. She had no verbal communication but would eye point to make choices. The class always used a visual timetable, which enabled children to understand the routine of the day. Gradually Rachel got less frustrated and even began trying to communicate with the other children in the class. By using eye pointing she was able to make her own choices of foods and drinks.

The staff soon discovered that Rachel loved listening to singing – although she was unable to sing along she would smile and dance whilst the songs were being sung, and after about six months was able to sit and listen to a story with a group of three children.

At the end of her first term Rachel took a very small part in the class nativity and her key worker from the previous nursery was invited by Rachel's parents, who were thrilled by the progress that she was making. Her key worker was delighted to see the changes and how content she now seemed.

Consider

- Why do you think that Rachel's progress had been so fast when starting school?
- What does this tell you about the benefits of special schools?
- What might some of the challenges be in special schools?

CURRICULUM

Recently changes to the curriculum (which were explained in Chapter 4) have had a really positive outcome for children in special schools. Previously the majority of children in special schools would have been working at P levels. These were used with children aged from five to sixteen who were struggling to meet the targets of the National Curriculum. However, as explained in Chapter 4, new levels have been brought in and replaced with 'pre-key skills'. The head teacher and teacher who supported me with the writing of this chapter told me that these have been a real asset to the children in the school. When I asked how, they told me that it has meant that they are better able to use play to support children's learning. So for instance when focusing on money, more practical skills can be taught through play that encourage the changing of money in a shop; as the children get older they can be taken into cafés and shops to buy items, whereby they really experience the practical element of using money.

Again, in English activities the children no longer have to focus on phonics, which previously were way beyond the comprehension of many in the school, and now can focus more on singing, storytelling and the children's individual therapy aims and goals. This enabled the school to make some changes to the curriculum taught and to take steps to embed part of the Equals Curriculum (n.d.) into lessons (www.equals.co.uk). This curriculum follows principles that are developmental and bespoke to each individual child, taking into account targets set out in the child's EHCP. The curriculum covers all stages of education from early years to young people up to the age of 25, as suggested through the new Code of Practice (DFE and DOH, 2014).

WHAT ARE THE CHALLENGES OF SPECIAL SCHOOLS?

Having focused on the benefits of special schools, it is only right that there should be mention of some of the more challenging aspects of such provision. One of these is that often the schools are not within the community that the child lives in. This may mean that if a parent has two children in different schools the child with SEND will need to be transported by taxi. There is usually an escort who travels with the children and ensures that they are safe and happy. This can also impact the child's socialisation skills as they may have fewer opportunities for play dates and parties with friends they meet at school.

Some parents may also be put off by the slightly more limited curriculum, depending on the cognitive needs of the children. However, as has already been explained, special schools will offer a bespoke curriculum that meets the child's abilities and interests.

Finally there may be a stigma attached to attending special schools, which can be born out of ignorance or fear. However, I would encourage any student or volunteer to go and spend time in special schools to see how the children are cared for and educated in quite a unique way.

As a result of reading this chapter you will have:

- understood some of the political background of educational provision for children with SEND
- examined how mainstream schools can support children with SEND
- reflected on the inclusive nature, benefits and challenges of special schools.

The next chapter will bring the book to a close and set out what conclusions each chapter has drawn.

END OF CHAPTER QUESTIONS

- In what ways have you understood how choices of educational provision are linked to the medical and social models of disability?
- What are some of the benefits and challenges to the inclusion of children with SEND in mainstream schools?
- What is your view on whether special schools are inclusive?

FURTHER READING

Blackburn, C. (n.d.) Early care and education for young children born prematurely. bcuassets.blob.core.windows.net/docs/premature-birth-report-final-version-131564422587951922.pdf

Many children in special schools these days have been born prematurely and therefore have many and varied medical and learning needs. This article discusses the training needs of the practitioners who work with these children.

Runswick-Cole, K. (2008) Between a rock and a hard place: Parents' attitudes to the inclusion of children with special educational needs in mainstream and special schools. *British Journal of Special Education* 35 (3): 173–80.

This article discusses the dilemmas of parents who have to make the decision whether or not to send their child to a mainstream school with support or a special school.

Tutt, R. and Williams, P. (2015) *The SEND Code of Practice 0–25 Years – Policy, Provision and Practice.* London: Sage.

This textbook goes through the legislative requirements of the new SEND Code of Practice.

8

CONCLUSION

In this conclusion each chapter will be summarised and it will include some discussion and thoughts of the main points mentioned in the chapter. It will also include in-text citations, some of which may appear in previous chapters but some may be new. These might be useful for you to access if you want to undertake further research.

By the end of this chapter you will have:

- understood how all the chapters in the book link with each other
- discovered the importance of inclusion to the lives of children with SEND
- examined the challenging aspect of the 'unique child' in the EYFS in the 21st century.

CHAPTER 1 - LEGISLATION AND POLICY IN RELATION TO SPECIAL NEEDS

This chapter draws together information around the importance of policies in practice and how they shape provision, particularly for children with SEND. The chapter begins by setting out the importance of legislation and how policy is often related to what is going on in society, both internationally and nationally. In terms of SEND, one of the reasons why policy has changed so much recently is because, and rightly so, more children are being diagnosed with SEND at an earlier age, and they and their families need services that meet their requirements. The chapter discusses the various levels of policy making and how new policies are cascaded down by local authorities to ensure that settings are working appropriately to support children with SEND. Differing perspectives on SEND are offered to help the reader to recognise that there are many views on education and that these contrasting views can support and challenge our thinking.

The medical and social models of disability are introduced in order to increase your understanding of how educational provision has changed over the years but to also support the reader to see that some elements of the medical model still exist in current practice.

We read how at the end of the 19th century it was common for children with SEND to be taught in institutions away from their homes, by low-skilled practitioners who had never received any appropriate training. These institutions remained until the groundbreaking review of provision was carried out by Mary Warnock in 1978. Warnock's work made very significant changes when she recommended that children with SEND should be taught in their local community schools rather than in institutions as they had previously been.

The chapter discusses how in the 1990s two international treaties were introduced which revolutionised practice for children across the world, particularly those with SEND. Both the United Nations Convention on the Rights of the Child (UNICEF, 1989) and the Salamanca Statement (UNESCO, 1994) established that children with disabilities should be educated in their community primary schools. Both statements discuss the importance of a child's voice and that their needs should always be taken into account when considering their educational provision. However, these documents are not legally binding and they have their critics, who state that they are written from the perspective of the developed world rather than the developing world (Borkett, 2018).

The chapter then discusses more recent policies, including the National Curriculum and the slightly contentious concept of a curriculum for the youngest children – the Early Years Foundation Stage. However, at the time of its inception increasing numbers of parents were returning to work after having children and so childcare became more in demand. The establishment of the Curriculum Guidance for the Foundation Stage was an opportunity to set priorities and standards for those practitioners working with the youngest children.

The chapter then discusses how this curriculum, which brought with it the concept of the 'unique child', shaped provision until 2019. Currently a consultation into changes to the curriculum, to be brought in in 2020, is being carried out – only time will tell what changes this will bring.

The chapter then discussed the Special Educational Needs Codes of Practice set up by the Department for Education and Skills in 2001 and the second one by the Department of Health and Department of Education in 2014. These established that all children with disabilities should be issued with a statement of educational needs known now as an Education, Health Care Plan (EHCP), which sets out what the child's needs are and how they should be addressed through education and other services. It also identifies areas of support for the family. As with many areas of legislation, there were people who felt that such statements were not inclusive as they set out what the child could not do rather than first and foremost looking at what they could achieve.

CHAPTER 2 - THE DILEMMA THAT IS INCLUSION

At the heart of this book is the concept of inclusion and the need to view the uniqueness of all children and the families/carers who they grow up with. The chapter starts with consideration of groups of people that are excluded in society. When we ourselves have experienced exclusion it is sometimes easier to understand how others may feel when they are excluded day after day, week after week, month after month, year after year. It is useful when focusing on those who are excluded to consider what it is that excludes children. In the chapter there is mention of the standards-driven educational system in the UK which excludes children with SEND who are not allowed into certain schools as it may lower the league tables. There is also consideration of the entrance requirements of some private schools, which exclude children with SEND by being so high and completely unattainable. It was interesting to read in the media about vulnerable children with SEND who had been taken out of schools for varying reasons for months and at times years (Weale and McIntyre, 2018) due to a lack of funding for children with SEND. In September of this year Sellgren from the BBC made the suggestion that children who do not yet have Education, Health Care Plans are 'particularly exposed and more likely to be excluded from schools' (Sellgren, 2019). These issues demonstrate that inclusion is certainly not working in some areas of the country due to local authority setbacks, which as Jayanetti (2018) suggests are partly due to austerity.

The chapter also focused on how inclusion has evolved over the years. Twenty years ago it was in the main related to children with SEND, but now, in line with the Equality Act 2010, it relates also to gender, culture, faith, sexuality and medical needs. It is a principle that means different things to different people and there is discussion of the many and varied definitions of inclusion. Issues around the differences between integration and inclusion were also covered. In the past, education took more of an integrated approach whereby the child had to fit into the school so the schools did not need to make many changes to accommodate the needs of the child. However, now schools are expected to make 'reasonable adjustments' to ensure that children with SEND are able to attend their local mainstream schools, but it is left to the discretion of the head teacher as to what those adjustments might be.

CASE STUDY 8.1

Joel

Joel had moderate learning difficulties and behavioural issues and was supported by a teaching assistant (TA) three days a week. His parents' marriage had broken down recently but they were still living together as they felt their children would be less affected by the breakup if they continued this pattern of life. Joel struggled to communicate and so used Makaton to support his language, but if he was upset or stressed he could become quite violent and would hit the children around him. One day a dance group were coming to Joel's school to work with children who had specific emotional issues. They were doing mindfulness, yoga and relaxation activities. Joel's Mum was keen that he should be included as it could help him to regulate his own behaviour a little. The head teacher was not so keen as she was concerned that it might spark some negative behaviour. Joel's TA accompanied him to the session and it went well. Joel relaxed and joined in and some of the programmes were used afterwards to support Joel's emotional wellbeing.

Consider

- What would have been your reaction in this circumstance?
- Which policies would the school have been going against by not letting Joel go to the session?
- How in particular do you think the session benefited Joel?

The final section of this chapter focused on what practitioners can do to ensure that their practice is inclusive, particularly for children with SEND. My belief is that whatever practitioners can do to improve provision for children with SEND will make things better and more inclusive for all. The chapter considered the need for the environment to be welcoming, including pictures of a range of children, and calming colours that are more subdued as bright colours can sometimes overstimulate children. Natural resources support children's natural curiosity and, as was noted in Chapter 7, can encourage them to explore, develop and learn at a deeper level. It is also important that children in settings have the opportunity to communicate with each other, and as this can be an area that some children find particularly stressful, it is vital that a range of augmentative communication systems are available. Signing such as Makaton or British Sign Language for those who are deaf can really support young children's speaking skills; Picture Exchange Communication Systems can also support children who, with the addition of pictures and words, can begin to make the links between something and the need to ask for it. Computers can support some children in their language skills. Children can become very stressed and feel very vulnerable when they are unable to make their views and needs known, so it is vital that they should be supported to communicate in settings.

CHAPTER 3 - EARLY INTERVENTION

This chapter discussed the importance of early intervention for children who are either born with a disability or for whom a disability is suspected but not yet diagnosed. The chapter begins by looking at the evolution of such programmes and again recognises that initially early intervention programmes were for children with SEND but more recently have become programmes for those with communication problems, sensory impairments including autism, physical difficulties and behavioural problems, as well as parenting support.

The work of Urie Bronfenbrenner is introduced, which is known as the ecological systems theory. This demonstrates how the child is at the centre of four different systems. All levels interact with each other and can therefore have various effects on the family and child. I believe this to be a really good tool which can support practitioners in understanding how, if one element of a child's life is affected by something, it may also affect other areas too. This was demonstrated by the case study in the previous section of this conclusion. The child had problems with his communication but his parents' breakup was also having a negative effect on the child's behaviour.

The chapter then goes on to introduce some of the early intervention programmes that are used today in the UK. These are very effective and it is important to note that interventions offered to the young early on in their lives can mean there will be huge savings financially as the child grows (HM Government, 2011). This report also points out that those families living in areas of deprivation are less likely to do well educationally compared with their peers living in more affluent areas. The chapter discusses the work of the Labour government in introducing Sure Start centres to the UK in 2011. These set out to try to ensure that young children were better supported and that parents were introduced to the best way to encourage their children's development and learning.

The final section of the chapter focused on the benefits and challenges of early intervention programmes particularly to parents.

CHAPTER 4 – ASSESSMENT AND OBSERVATION FOR CHILDREN WITH SPECIAL EDUCATIONAL NEEDS AND DISABILITY

This chapter discussed the sometimes controversial place of assessment and how this can support children with SEND. It is controversial because there are many people who believe that there is too much reliance on assessment in the British education system and that it has become too bureaucratic, especially for children in the early years. Lawlor (2019), writing on behalf of the Early Years Alliance, states the need for assessment to become less bureaucratic and to be more about teachers' knowledge and engagement with children and what they know.

There are many different assessments that children with SEND may go through depending on what agency is involved, and this can make the whole process very time-consuming and repetitive for parents; however, some of these are necessary before a diagnosis can be made.

The chapter goes on to explore what both the SEND Code of Practice (DFE and DOH, 2014) and the Early Years Foundation Stage (EYFS) (DCSF, 2008) say about the place of assessment for children with SEND. It discusses the two levels of support for those children: the Education, Health and Care Plan (EHCP), which replaced the Statement of Educational Needs in 2014, and the role of SEN support for those who have not yet got a statement. The chapter also discusses the role of the Special Educational Needs Co-ordinator (SENCO) and changes made to this role since 2014 when the new Code of Practice was introduced. Again, some have talked of the changes to this role and how it too has become more strategic (Hunt and Newbold, 2018).

CASE STUDY 8.2

Beth

Beth worked as a SENCO in a private day nursery. She had worked there since 2009 and had supported many children over the years. She had accessed training wherever possible as she wanted to ensure that all children received the best support that they could. Beth had also accessed training from the Portage Association, which had supported her knowledge of working with children with SEND. Beth's role at the setting also included support for parents of children, especially through the assessment process of diagnosis and statementing.

Beth was aware of the fact that there were to be changes made to the old SEN Code of Practice, but was shocked by the implications of the new Code for her role as a SENCO when it was launched in 2014. The new Code stated that SENCOs should ideally have a master's level qualification, and that their role was to include working with the other agencies involved with the child and family and consulting with the child's key worker about what support the child could access in the setting.

Beth had a Foundation Degree in Early Years but was not yet at master's level in her training. As the setting was private it meant that in future the SENCO support that they accessed should now come from someone employed by the local authority. Whilst the local authority's SENCO had previously visited the setting, it was really only to ensure that all the children with SEND were adequately supported.

The setting now had to get used to a new way of working as well as receiving more support from the local authority's SENCO. However, she had no links with the families involved and only visited the setting once every half-term. The nursery decided that their old way of working was best and continued with Beth supporting the families. They felt that this gave a more personalised support to families and children.

Consider

- How do you view the new role of the SENCO?

- What might be the benefits of someone with a master's level qualification in the SENCO role?

- What might the challenges be of a master's level qualification in the SENCO role?

- What are the benefits and challenges of these changes to parents?

Links to the curriculum are further discussed, and the chapter introduces recent changes made – in the light of the Rochford Review – to P scales, which were previously used by practitioners to ascertain the levels at which children with SEND were learning.

The final part of this chapter focused on the role of observation and how this links to assessment. It explores the different ways of and reasons for observation and how they can support practitioners to evaluate the development and learning of young children with SEND.

CHAPTER 5 - THE AMBIGUITIES OF PLAY

I see this as a really important chapter in the book. Practitioners are taught about the value of play at all levels of training and continue to be educated in the many theories that suggest children develop and learn through play. Yet often when I asked students coming onto the Foundation Degree what role they took, they would respond 'I am just a nursery nurse and I play with children all day' in a slightly bored tone. Of course I would quickly retaliate that this is one of the most important things that practitioners do with young children, but they would respond that parents often did not understand why play was important. So I felt a chapter relating to play was very important in this book.

The chapter discussed firstly some of the policies that point out the importance of play in children's lives. This gives the chapter an international foundation which firmly makes the case that children have the right to play and for that play to support a child's development and learning. The chapter introduces the work of the National Portage Association (NPA), who train early years practitioners to deliver Portage in the homes of very young children with SEND. The programme has at its heart the belief that children learn through play.

The chapter then moves on to try and define what play is – this is another of those principles that means different things to different people and will vary depending on where in the world you might come from. However, this in itself demonstrates what a complex principle it is – it is something that has always challenged me as both a student and a lecturer.

One of the other reasons for writing this chapter was because I have often heard practitioners stating that children with SEND do not know how to play. To a certain degree this is correct, but I think there are reasons for this which are more to do with their cognitive skills and the fact that they often do not understand the purpose of toys unless a practitioner has modelled the play before-hand. In my view practitioners should be facilitators or partners in play and it is part of their role to get alongside children and play with them. This can, however, be a challenge if you are working with children on the autistic spectrum who may also struggle to play or can become quite obsessive about activities such as spinning wheels and lining up cars. Here it is important that practitioners should follow their lead in play by copying them and allowing them to be 'leaders of their play' whilst using simple words that describe what is going on.

The chapter then discusses various theorists who have tried to determine how it is that children play, develop and learn. The works of Froebel, Montessori and Goldschmied were examined, particularly because their theories relate to the use of natural objects and resources, which ignite children's innate curiosity. The chapter also introduced the work of Rogoff who, like Vygotsky and Bruner, views the social element of a child's life as an essential part of their learning but also recognises that the culture a child grows up in can have an impact on their development and learning. This suggests that children do not just learn by play but they also learn from their social world, their conversations and the people they share their lives with.

The final section of this chapter focused on the role of the practitioner in setting up inclusive environments that relate to all children and that contain a number of sensory activities, which are enjoyable. Children naturally love exploration, and so it is vital that they have the opportunity to investigate different textures and resources.

CHAPTER 6 – PARTNERSHIPS WITH PARENTS AND FAMILIES

The chapter starts with discussion of the evolving nature of parental involvement in education. The EYFS states that 'parents are a child's first educators'

(DCSF, 2008), implying therefore that it is to be expected that parents should become involved in their child's education. However, depending on your own experience of being parented and on the individual needs of your child, this can prove challenging. The chapter discusses the multi-agency notion of working as a team and the importance of this to parents and families in order to prevent them from feeling ostracised or indeed silenced.

The chapter moves on to discuss how parents relate to the diagnosis of a SEND and the effect that this can have on both parents and the wider family and community. This can lead the parents to go through a period of grieving for the child that they were expecting to have who now has a 'label' of some kind of disability. It can also mean that each time a child goes through a 'rite of passage' those feelings of grief may re-emerge. However, once the child has received a diagnosis, parents are then better able to access financial assistance through benefits, have the exact cause of a child's disability written into their EHCP, or if the child has not yet got one can be issued with an EHCP and can access more support through different agencies. During this difficult process parents require practitioners who can support them sensitively, with empathy and compassion.

The final section focused on the role of the family and how this has changed, particularly over the past 50 years. This can have an impact on practitioners, families and children. It may mean that practitioners need to be challenged away from what may be old stereotypical views of the role of the family to consider new and different ways of being parents. This section also focused on the impact on the grandparents and siblings of having a child with a disability. This, as I discovered, is an area where little research has been done, therefore there was not a lot of information to draw on; but what I did find illustrates that they too need a lot of support, both in accepting a diagnosis and in relation to the caring aspect of having a child with a disability.

CHAPTER 7 - EDUCATIONAL PROVISION FOR CHILDREN WITH SPECIAL EDUCATIONAL NEEDS AND DISABILITY

This chapter begins by focusing on the political background of educational provision and how it has changed over the years, particularly for the needs of children with SEND who previously would have been educated in institutions. Now with the introduction of the Children and Families Act 2014 and the SEND Code of Practice 2014, parents have a greater right to choose where they want their child to be educated and for that setting to accept their child, providing they feel that they are able to do this appropriately. The chapter revisits the medical and social models of disability and explains how these have affected educational provision over the years.

The chapter then moves on to discuss both mainstream provision, including enhanced resource units which are thought by some to be a bridge between mainstream and special education (Tutt and Williams, 2015), and special provision, which incorporates the three types of education for children with SEND in the UK. It focuses on both the benefits and the challenges of each, and discusses why it is that parents choose one or the other for their child. It also explores whether special schools are inclusive and how they offer a bespoke curriculum for children that is, where appropriate, more play related and based around life skills.

A FINAL THOUGHT

During the writing of this book I have read many chapters, articles and papers relating to children with SEND and this has led me to re-examine my own views on certain aspects of it. These final paragraphs will discuss some of the thoughts that have emerged over the past 18 months.

It is good to see that over the years international, national and local policies relating to children with SEND have, in the main, related to the inclusion of children with special needs in mainstream wherever possible. This is a really positive aspect of educational provision in the UK. However, if inclusion is truly to be the ideal that so many hope for, it needs to be endorsed with a commitment from whichever government is in power for better training of practitioners, better salaries for the early years workforce and a greater understanding of the needs of children with disabilities.

I make no apologies that at the heart of this book is inclusion, for this is as it should be. I believe that, at the very heart of all phases of education, from the early years into further and higher education, children and young people should have the opportunity to experience inclusion. It is especially important as part of the foundation stone of children's lives that they grow up to view difference as exciting and stimulating rather than viewing it in a negative way. However, in order to be effective it needs an infrastructure that is supportive and is prepared to meet the individual needs of every child. Whilst the neoliberal stance of government continues to be about targets, standards and competition, I do not believe that inclusion will be appropriate for every child.

Throughout the book I have talked of the importance of play and I continue to believe in the transformative nature of this. However, I meet practitioners who have little awareness of the importance of it or how it can impact on young children in many ways, and this concerns me. It is vital that practitioners coming to work with young children in the 21st century receive training relating to the importance of all types of play. However, I do think at times that we need to be a little more understanding of parents who may come from different parts of the world or those who do not value the importance of play because they would prefer their children to read and write. It is about getting alongside parents and understanding where their views come from, and then gently working with them to see that through play children learn so much.

Finally, a word to the many practitioners who work every day to support all children. I have always really liked the term 'the unique child' in the EYFS and valued what it says about seeing every child as an individual with different abilities, fascinations and ways of learning. However, recently I have begun to wonder how much notice politicians, practitioners and parents really take of this ideal. Elements of children's uniqueness have a huge impact on their identity. Aspects such as gender, abilities, culture, faith, language and fascinations all have a huge impact on children's identity and how children see themselves, but I am not sure that this is supported by all practitioners. Please, practitioners, make the time to find out about children and their families in a positive way – value them and all that they bring into your setting. To end this book I will use the quotation that I used at the beginning:

> Remember that everyone is a human being. Value every child for who they are. Start with what they can do, not what they can't... Never consider there is an alternative; every child is entitled to a preschool place. (Purdue, 2009: 142)

REFERENCES

Adams, C. (2012) The history of health visiting. www.nursinginpractice.com/article/his tory-health-visiting

Ailwood, J. (2003) Governing early childhood education through play. *Contemporary Issues in Early Childhood* 4 (3): 286–99.

Ainscow, M. (2000) Breaking down the barriers: The Index of Inclusion. *Center for Studies on Inclusive Education.* www.csie.org.uk/resources/breaking-barriers

Allan, J. (2010) The sociology of disability and the struggle for inclusive education. *British Journal of Sociology of Education* 31 (5): 603–19.

Allan, J. and Slee, R. (2008) *Doing Inclusive Education Research.* Rotterdam: Sense.

Allen, G. (2011) *Early Intervention: The Next Steps.* www.gov.uk/government/publica tions/early-intervention-the-next-steps--2

Ang, L. (2014) Preschool or prep school? Rethinking the role of early years education. *Journal of Contemporary Issues in Early Childhood* 15 (2): 185–99.

Armstrong, F. (2002) The historical development of special education: Humanitarian rationality or 'wild profusion of entangled events'? *History of Education* 31(5): 437–56.

Atkinson, C., Bond, C., Goodhall, N. and Woods, F. (2017) Children's access to their right to play: Findings from two exploratory studies. *Educational & Child Psychology* 34 (3): 20–36.

Avramidis, E., Bayliss, P. and Burden, R. (2000) A survey into mainstream teachers' attitudes towards the inclusion of children with special educational needs in the ordinary school in one local education authority. *International Journal of Educational Psychology* 20 (2): 191–211.

Bailey, J. (2016) What is augmentative and alternative communication? *ASHA.* www. asha.org/public/speech/disorders/AAC/k

Baldock, P. (2010) *Understanding Cultural Diversity in the Early Years.* London: Sage.

Baldock, P., Fitzgerald, D. and Kay J. (2013) *Understanding Early Years Policy* (3rd edn). London: Sage.

Barnardo's (2001) *A Review of Key Worker Systems for Disabled Children and the Development of Information Guides for Parents, Children and Professionals.* Policy and Research Unit. www.barnardos.org.uk/key_worker_full_report_wales.pdf

Barnardo's (2011) *The Value of Early Intervention.* www.barnardos.org.uk/what_we_do/ policy_research_unit/research_and_publications/the-value-of-early-intervention/ publication-view.jsp?pid=PUB-1860

Barton, L. (1987) *The Politics of Special Educational Needs.* Lewes: Falmer Press.

Barton, L. and Landman, M. (1993) The politics of integration: Observations on the Warnock Report. In: Slee, R. (ed.) *Is There a Desk with my Name on it? The Politics of Integration*. Abingdon: Routledge.

Basford, J. and Bath, C. (2014) Playing the assessment game: An English early childhood perspective. *International Journal of Early Years* 34 (2): 119–132.

Batorowicz, B., Stadskleiv, K., Von Tetzchner, S. and Missiuna, C. (2016) Children who use communication aids instructing peer and adult partners during play-based activity. *Augmentative and Alternative Communication* 32 (2): 105–19.

Beland, D., Cartensen, M.B. and Seabrook, L. (2016) Ideas, political power and public policy. *Journal of European Public Policy* 23 (3): 315–17.

Bercow, J. (2008) *The Bercow Report – A Review of Services for Children and Young People (0–19) with Speech, Language and Communication Needs*. www.dera.ioe.ac.uk/8405/

Blackburn, C. (n.d.) Early care and education for young children born prematurely. bcuassets.blob.core.windows.net/docs/premature-birth-report-final-version-131564 422587951922.pdf

Blann, L.E. (2005) Early intervention for children and families with special needs. *The Journal of Maternal/Child Nursing* 30 (4): 263–7.

Blunkett, D. and Rogers, L. (2015) *Making the Case for Play*. London: Sense. www.sense. org.uk/play

Booth, T. (2000) Inclusion and exclusion policy in England: Who controls the agenda? In: Armstrong, F., Armstrong, D. and Barton, L. (eds) *Inclusive Education – Policy, Contexts and Comparative Perspectives*. London: David Fulton.

Borkett, P.A. (2012) Diversity and inclusion in the early years. In: Kay, J. (ed.) *Good Practice in the Early Years*. London: Bloomsbury.

Borkett, P.A. (2018) *Cultural Diversity and Inclusion in Early Years Education*. Abingdon: Routledge.

Borkett, P.A. (2019) Inclusion and participation. In: Fitzgerald, D. and Maconochie, E. (eds) *Early Childhood Studies*. London: Sage.

Borsay, A. (2012) History and policy – Connecting historians, policy makers and the media. www.historyandpolicy.org/docs/dfe-anne-borsay-text.pdf

Boucher, S., Downing, J. and Shemilt, R. (2016) *The Role of Play in Children's Palliative Care*. United States National Library of Medicine.

Boyle, C., Scriven, B., Durning, S. and Downes, C. (2011) Facilitating the learning of all students: The 'professional positive' of inclusive practice in Australian primary schools. *Nasen British Journal of Learning Support* 26: 72–78.

Brewer, E. (2016) Nature is the best way to nurture pupils with SEN. *The Guardian*. www.theguardian.com/teacher-network/2016/may/01/nature-nurture-pupils-special-educational-needs-outdoor-education

Bridle, L. and Mann, G. (2000) *Mixed feelings: A parental perspective on early intervention*. Paper presented at the National Conference of Early Childhood Intervention, Brisbane, Australia.

British Broadcasting Corporation (BBC) (2014) How is the National Curriculum changing? www.bbc.co.uk/news/education-28989714

British Broadcasting Corporation (BBC) (2019) 'Unprecedented' levels of special needs complaints upheld. www.bbc.co.uk/news/education-49924189

British Broadcasting Corporation (BBC) (n.d.) Getting started with Makaton. www.bbc. co.uk/cbeebies/joinin/something-special-getting-started-with-makaton

Brock, A., Dodds, S., Jarvis, P. and Olusoga, Y. (2009) *Perspectives on Play – Learning for Life*. London: Pearson.

Brodie, K. (n.d.) Making observations. www.teachearlyyears.com/nursery-management/view/making-observations

Brodie, K. and Savage, K. (eds) (2015) *Inclusion and Early Years Practice*. Abingdon: Routledge.

Brooker, L. (2016) Childminders, parents and policy: Testing the triangle of care. *Journal of Early Childhood Research* 14 (1): 69–83.

Bruce, T. (2011) *Learning Through Play: For Babies, Toddlers and Young Children* (2nd edn). London: Hodder.

Bryan, J. (2017) I talk with my eyes. *The Guardian*. www.theguardian.com/lifeand style/2017/jan/27/experience-i-talk-with-my-eyes

Burman, E. (2008) *Deconstructing Developmental Psychology* (2nd edn). Abingdon: Routledge.

Carpenter, B. (2005) Early childhood intervention: Possibilities and prospects for professionals, families and children. *British Journal of Special Education* 32 (4): 176–83.

Carr, M. (2001) *Assessment in Early Childhood Settings: Learning Stories*. London: Sage.

Centre for Studies on Inclusive Education (CSIE) (2002) *Index for Inclusion – Developing Learning and Participation in Schools*. Bristol: CSIE.

Centre for Studies on Inclusive Education (CSIE) (2004) *Index for Inclusion – Developing Learning, Participation and Play in Early Years and Childcare*. Bristol: CSIE.

Centre for Studies on Inclusive Education (CSIE) (2018) The Unesco Salamanca Statement. www.csie.org.uk/inclusion/unesco-salamanca.shtml

Chambers, J. (2012) *A Sociology of Family Life – Changes and Diversity in Intimate Relations*. Cambridge: Polity Press.

Children and Families Act (2014) www.legislation.gov.uk/ukpga/2014/6/contents/enacted

Children's Commissioner (2012) *Annual Report*. www.childrenscommissioner.gov.uk/report/annual-report-2012-13/

Children's Society (2018) Work to secure more funding for local children's services. www.childrenssociety.org.uk/good-childhood-campaign/frequently-asked-questions?gclid=EAIaIQobChMIwcSfuemm3wIVU-d3Ch1v2AeUEAAYASAAEgInGfD_BwE

Children's Workforce Development Council (2009) The team around the child (TAC) and the lead professional. info@cwdcouncil.org.uk

Clark, A. and Moss, P. (2001) *The Mosaic Approach*. London: National Children's Bureau.

Coffey, C. (2013) The pros and cons of labelling a child with a developmental delay. www.thejournal.ie/readme/column-the-pros-and-cons-of-labelling-a-child-with-developmental-delay

Coles, E., Cheyne, H. and Daniel, B. (2015) Early years interventions to improve child health and wellbeing: What works for whom and in what circumstances? *Systematic Reviews* 6 (4): 79. www.ncbi.nlm.nih.gov/pubmed/26047950www.ncbi.nlm.nih.gov/pubmed/26047950

Collins, J. (2003) Exclusion: A silent protest. In: Nind, M., Sheehy, K. and Simmons, K. (eds) *Inclusive Education: Learners and Learning Contexts*. London: David Fulton.

Communication Matters (2018) Using objects of reference. www.makaton.org/about Makaton/

Community Playthings (n.d.) Heuristic play. www.communityplaythings.co.uk/learning-library/articles/heuristic-play

Connor, M. (1997) Parental motivation for specialist or mainstream placement. *Support for Learning* 12 (3).

Contact for Families with Disabled Children (2019) What to expect at an assessment. contact.org.uk/advice-and-support/social-care/how-to-access-services/needs-assessments

Cooper, L. and Harlow, J. (2018) Physical development. In: Johnston, J., Nahmad-Williams, L., Oates, R. and Wood, V. (eds) *Early Childhood Studies – Principles and Practice*. Abingdon: Routledge.

Coram Children's Legal Centre (CCLC) (2016) Permanent and fixed period exclusion of children aged 3–7 from maintained schools and academes. www.coram.org.uk/how-we-do-it/coram-childrens-legal-centre-upholding-childrens-rights

Corbett, J. (1996) *Bad-Mouthing: The Language of Special Needs*. London: The Falmer Press.

Council for Disabled Children (n.d. a) Early support: an integrated and person centred approach. https://councilfordisabledchildren.org.uk/our-work/whole-child/practice/early-support-integrated-and-person-centered-approach

Council for Disabled Children (n.d. b) Local offer – what is a local offer? councilford isabledchildren.org.uk/sites/default/files/uploads/resources/images/a4l-letlocalofferfinal7.pdf

Council for the Curriculum, Examinations & Assessment. (2016). Types of Assessment. Available at: www.ccea.or.uk/curriculum/assess_progress?types_assessment

Crutchley, R. (2018) Legislation and policy: toward a participatory partnership. In: Crutchley, R. (ed.) *Special Needs in the Early Years*. London: Sage.

Crutchley, R. and Hunt, R. (2018) Early intervention and transition. In: Crutchley, R. (ed.) *Special Needs in the Early Years: Partnership and Participation*. London: Sage

Daniels, K. and Taylor, R. (2019) Children as learners: Multimodal perspectives on play and learning. In: Fitzgerald, D. and Maconochie, E. (eds) *Early Childhood Studies – A Student's Guide*. London: Sage.

Department for Children, Schools and Families (DCSF) (2008) *The Early Years Foundation Stage*. Nottingham: DCSF Publications.

Department for Education (DFE) (2011) *National Evaluation of Sure Start*. www.gov.uk/government/publications/national-evaluation-of-sure-start-local-programmes-an-economic-perspective

Department for Education (DFE) (2012) *New research shows early intervention is key in helping children with special needs*. www.gov.uk/government/news/new-research-shows-early-intervention-is-key-in-helping-children-with-special-needs

Department for Education (DFE) (2015) Area guidelines for SEND and alternative provision including special schools, alternative provision, specially resourced provision and units. www.asscts.publishing.service.gov.uk/government/uploads/system/uploads/attachment_data/file/719176/Building_Bulletin_104_Area_guidelines_f

Department for Education (DFE) (2017) Early Years Foundation Stage. www.gov.uk

Department for Education (DFE) (2018a) A *Celebratory Approach to SEND Assessment in the Early Years*. HYPERLINK "http://www.pengreen.org/wp-content/uploads/2018/05/" www.pengreen.org/wp-content/uploads/2018/05/ A-Celebratory-Approach-to-SEND-Assessment in-the-Early-Years.pdf

Department for Education (DFE) (2018b) SEND in England. HYPERLINK "http://www.assets.publishingser/" www.assets.publishingservice.gov.uk/governmentuploads/.../SEN-2018

Department for Education (DFE) (2018c) Sure Start. www.education-ni.gov.uk/articles/sure-start

Department for Education (DFE) (2018d) Permanent and fixed period exclusions in England: 2016–2017. Darlington. www.gov.uk/government/statistics/permanent-and-fixed-period-exclusions-in-england-2016-to-2017

Department for Education and Department of Health (DFE and DOH) (2014) *Special Educational Needs and Disability Code of Practice: 0–25 Years*. www.gov.uk/government/publications/send-code-of-practice-0-to-25

Department for Education and Employment/Qualifications and Curriculum Authority (DFEE/QCA) (2000) *Curriculum Guidance for the Foundation Stage*. London: DFEE.

Department for Education and Skills (DFES) (2001) *Special Educational Needs – Code of Practice*. Nottingham: DFES. www.gov.uk/government/publications/special-educational-needs-sen-code-of-practice

Department for Education and Skills (DFES) (2004) *Removing the Barriers to Achievement: The Government's Strategy for SEN*. London: DFES.

Dickens, J. (2017). Conservative manifesto: The full list of schools policies. schoolsweek.co.uk/conservative-manifesto-the-full-list-of-schools-policies/

disabilitynottinghamshire (n.d.) The social model vs the medical model of disability. www.disabilitynottinghamshire.org.uk/about/social-model-vs-medical-model-of-disability/

Douglas, M. (1996) *Purity and Danger: An Analysis of the Concepts of Pollution and Taboo*. Abingdon: Routledge.

Dowling, M. (2006) *Supporting Young Children's Sustained Shared Thinking; An Exploration* (Training Materials). London: Early Education.

Dunn, K. (2000) Perspectives of non-disabled children on their disabled siblings. In: Moore, M. (ed.) *Insider Perspectives on Inclusion – Raising Voices, Raising Issues*. Sheffield: Philip Armstrong.

Early Education (DU) *About Froebel*. https://www.early-education.org.uk/about-froebel

Early Education (2012a) *Characteristics of Effective Learning*. www.foundationyears.org.uk/.../Development-Matters-FINAL-PRINT-AMEND

Early Education (2019) Getting it right in the EYFS means looking at the evidence. www.early-education.org.uk/getting_it_right_in_the-EYFS

Early Intervention Foundation (2015) *Social and emotional skills in childhood and their long-term effects on adult life*. https://www.eif.org.uk/report/social-and-emotional-skills-in-childhood-and-their-long-term-effects-on-adult-life

Early Intervention Foundation (2018) *Realising the Potential of Early Intervention*. London: Early Intervention Foundation.

Education Act (1996) www.legislation.gov.uk/ukpga/1996/56/contents

Education in England (2012) *The Warnock Report: Special Educational Needs*. www.educationengland.org.uk/documents/warnock/

Education-Line (2008) *Tears of the Phoenix: How nurturing and support became the 'cure' for further education*. Paper presented at BERA Conference, Edinburgh.

Edwards, M. and Davison, C. (eds) (2015) *Global Childhoods*. Norwich: Critical Publishing.

Emmons, P.G. and Anderson, L.M. (2005) *Understanding Sensory Dysfunction: Learning, Development and Sensory Dysfunction in Autism Spectrum Disorders, ADHD, Learning Disabilities and Bipolar Disorder*. London: Jessica Kingsley.

Equality Act (2010) www.legislation.gov.uk/ukpga/2010/15/contents

Equals Curriculum (n.d.) We support professionals working in the Special Educational Needs Sector (SEN). www://equals.co.uk/

European Agency for Special Needs and Inclusive Education (1998) Assessment in inclusive settings. www.europeanagency.org

European Commission. (2013). Support for children with SEN. ec.eurpoa.eu/social/BlobServelet?docld=15975&langld=en

Fisher, J. (2016) *Interacting or Interfering? Improving Interactions in the Early Years*. Milton Keynes: Open University Press.

Flandrin, L. (1979) *Families in Former Times*. Cambridge: Cambridge University Press.

Full Fact (2017) Grammar schools and social mobility: What's the evidence? https://fullfact.org/education/grammar-schools-and-social-mobility-whats-evidence/

Garner, R. (2008) More than 4,000 children under 5 excluded from school. *The Independent*. www.independent.co.uk/news/education/education-news/more-than-4000-children-under-five-excluded-from-school-998193.html?pageToolsFontSize=200%25

Gascoyne, S. (2012) *Treasure Baskets and Beyond – Realizing the Potential of Sensory-rich Play*. Milton Keynes: Open University Press..

Gascoyne, S. (2013) *Sensory Play. (Play in the EYFS)* (2nd edn). London: Practical Pre School.

Georgesen, J., Barr, V. and Mathers. S with Boag-Munroe, G., Parker-Rees, R. and Caruso, F. (2014) *Two Year Olds in England – An Exploratory Study*. Education Research with Plymouth University and the University of Oxford.

Gibbs, N. (2005) Parents behaving badly. *Time* 165 (8): 40–9.

Glass, C. (2000) *Working with Hannah: A Special Girl in a Mainstream School*. Abingdon: Routledge.

Gloucestershire.gov.uk (n.d.) The ABC of behaviour. www.gloucestershire.gov.uk/media/11951/behaviour-observation-sheets.pdf

Gold, A., Bowe, R. and Ball, S.J. (1993) Special educational needs in a new context: Micro politics, money and education for all. In: Slee, R. (ed.) *Is There a Desk with My Name on it? The Politics of Integration*. London: Routledge.

Godley, D. and Runswick-Cole. K. (2010) Emancipating play: Dis/abled children, development and deconstruction. *Disability & Society* 25 (4): 499–512.

Gov.UK (2010) The Equality Act. www.gov.uk/guidance/equality-act-2010-guidance

Gov.UK (n.d. a) Children with special educational needs and disabilities. www.gov.uk/children-with-special-educational-needs/extra-SEN-help

Gov.UK (n.d. b) Parental rights and responsibilities. www.gov.uk/parental-rights-responsibilities.

Gray, C. and Macblain, S. (2015) *Learning Theories in Childhood* (2nd edn). London: Sage.

Greene, V., Joshi, P., Street, C. and Soar, S. – National Children's Bureau (2015) *Two-Year-Olds in Schools: A Case Study of Eight Schools. A Research Report*. Department for Education. www.assets.publishing.service.gov.uk

Gregory, C. (2019) The five stages of grief – An examination of the Kübler-Ross model. www.psycom.net/depression.central.grief.html

Greishaber, S. and McArdle, F. (2010) *The Trouble with Play*. Maidenhead: Open University Press.

Gupta, S.S., Henninger, W.R. and Vinh, M.E. (eds) (2014) *First Steps to Pre-school Inclusion: How to Jumpstart Your Programwide Plan*. Baltimore, MD: Brookes.

Guralnick, M.J. (1989) Social competence as a future direction for early intervention programmes. *Journal of Mental Deficiency Research*, 33 (4): 275–81.

Hannahy, J. (2019) Joying with a new approach to play. *National Day Nurseries Association Quarterly Magazine*.

Hannon, P. and Fox, L. (2005) Why we should learn from Sure Start. In: Weinberger, J., Pickstone, C. and Hannon, P. (eds) *Learning from Sure Start – Working with Young Children and their Families*. Maidenhead: Open University Press.

Harris, J. (2018) The sinister segregation policies excluding children who don't fit in. *The Guardian.* https://www.theguardian.com/commentisfree/2018/apr/16/pupils-special-educational-needs-children-mainstream-schools

Hazell, W. (2017) SEND education 'too dependent on teaching assistants', researchers say. www.tes.com/news/send-education-too-dependent-teaching-assistants-researchers-say

Health Foundation (2018) *The Health Foundation's Submission: Response to the First 1000 Days of Life Inquiry.* www.health.org.uk/sites/default/files/2018-11/the_health_foundation_submission_to_first_1000_days_of_life_inquiry_-_hsc_committee_october_2018.pdf

Hellyn, L. and Bennett, S. (2017) *The A to Z of The Curiosity Approach.* Bedford: Diverze Print Ltd.

Henninger, W. and Gupta, S. (2014) How do children benefit from inclusion? In: Gupta, S.S., Henninger, W.R. and Vinh, M.E. (eds) *First Steps to Preschool Inclusion: How to Jumpstart Your Programwide Plan.* Baltimore, MD: Brookes.

Historic England (n.d.) Specialist education for children with disabilities – the happiest effect. historicengland.org.uk/research/inclusive-heritage/disability-history/1660-1832/specialist-education/

HM Government (2003) *Every Child Matters.* London: Her Majesty's Stationery Office.

HM Government (2011) Early intervention: Smart investment, massive savings. assets.publishing.service.gov.uk/government/uploads/system/uploads/attachment_data/file/61012/earlyintervention-smartinvestment.pdf

Hodge, N. (2005) Reflections on diagnosing autism spectrum disorders. www.shura.shu.ac.uk/information.html

Hornby, G. (2015) Inclusive special education: Development of a new theory for the education of children with special educational needs and disabilities. *British Journal of Special Education* 42 (3): 234–56.

House of Commons Library (2017) *Early Intervention.* Briefing Paper No. 7647. London: House of Commons. Available at: www.parliamen.uk/commons.library/intranet.parliament.uk/commons-library

House of Commons Science and Technology Committee (2018) *Evidence-based Early-years Intervention Inquiry – 11th Report of Session.* London: House of Commons.

Hughes, A. (n.d.). Rediscovered treasure – Elinor Goldschmied's treasure basket. www.froebel.org.uk/resources/elinor-goldschmied-s-treasure-basket/

Hunt, R. (2018) Models of SEN provision: The inclusion debate. In: Crutchley, R. (ed.) *Special Needs in the Early Years – Partnership and Participation.* London: Sage.

Hunt, R. and Newbold, A. (2018) CPD opportunities for staff working with children with SEND in the early years. In: Crutchley, R. (ed.) *Special Needs in the Early Years – Partnership and Participation.* London: Sage.

I CAN (2018) Supporting the lost generation. www.ican.org.uk/bercow-ten-years-on/

Independent Provider of Special Education Advice (IPSEA) (n.d.) What does SEN support in school mean? www.ipsea.org.uk/faqs/what-does-sen-support-in-school-mean

Institute for Education (2004) *Removing the Barriers to Achievement.* dera.ioe.ac.uk/4955/13/8b56f1b2944d88f593e89ae3009fa5c3_Redacted.pdf

International Play Association (IPA) (2010) *Promoting the Child's Right to Play.* IPA Global Consultations on Children's Rights to Play Report. Farringdon: IPA.

International Play Association (2014) The child's rights to play. www.ipaworld.org/childs-right-to-play/the-childs-right-to-play/

Jayanetti, C. (2018) Austerity cuts force special needs children into isolation. www.politics. co.uk/comment-analysis/2018/03/12/austerity-cuts-force-special-needs-children-in-to-isolation

Jones, F., Pring, T. and Grove, N. (2002) Developing communication in adults with profound and multiple learning difficulties using objects of reference. *International Journal of Language Communication Disorders* 37 (2): 173–84.

Jones, K. (2016) *Education in Britain – 1944 to the Present.* Cambridge: Polity Press.

Joseph Rowntree Foundation (2016) *Special Education Needs and their Links to Poverty.* www.jrf.org.uk/report/special-educational-needs-and-their-links-poverty

Kagan, C., Lewis, S., Heaton, P. and Cranshaw, M. (1999) Enabled or disabled? Working parents of disabled children and the provision of child-care. *Journal of Community & Applied Social Psychology* 9: 369–81.

Kay, E., Tisdall, M., Davis, J.M., Hill, M. and Prout, A. (eds) (2006) *Children, Young People and Social Inclusion.* Bristol: The Policy Press.

Lawlor, R. (2019) Consultation on proposed changes to the EYFS open. www.eyalliance. org.uk/news/2019/10/consultation-proposed-changes-eyfs-opens

Levin, P. (1997) *Making Social Policy: The Mechanisms of Government and Politics to Investigate Them.* Buckingham: Open University Press.

Levitas, R. (1998) *The Inclusive Society? Social Exclusion and New Labour.* Basingstoke: Macmillan.

Levitas, R., Pantazis, C., Fahmy, E., Gordon, D., Lloyd, E. and Patsios, D. (2007) *The Multidimensional Analysis of Social Exclusion.* Project Report. Bristol: University of Bristol.

Lewis, P.J. (2017) The erosion of play. *International Journal of Play* 6 (1): 10–23.

Liberal Democrats (2017) Demand better for our schools. www.libdems.org.uk/ education

Lindon, J. (2012) *Equality and Inclusion in Early Childhood* (2nd edn). Abingdon: Hodder.

Long, R. and Roberts, N. (2019) *Special Educational Needs: Support in England.* Briefing Paper No. 07020. www.parliament.uk/commons-library

Lowes, L. and Lyne, P. (2001) Chronic sorrow in parents of children with newly diagnosed diabetes: A review of the literature and discussion of the implications for nursing practice. *Journal of Advanced Nursing* 32 (1): 41–8.

Macblain, S., Dunn, J. and Luke, I. (2017) *Contemporary Childhood.* London: Sage.

MacNaughton, G. and Hughes, P. (2011) *Parents and Professionals in Early Childhood Settings.* Maidenhead: Open University Press.

MacNaughton, G., Rolfe, S. and Siraj-Blatchford, I. (eds) (2004) *Doing Early Childhood Research: International perspectives on Theory and Practice.* Buckingham: Open University Press.

Maconochie, E. and Branch, J. (2018) Working with families and professionals from other agencies. In: Fitzgerald, D. and Maconochie, E. (eds) *Early Childhood Studies – A Student's Guide.* London: Sage.

Makaton (2017) About Makaton. www.makaton.org/aboutMakaton/

McCoy, S. and Banks, J. (2012) Simply academic? Why children with special educational needs don't like school. *European Journal of Special Needs Education* 27 (1): 81–97.

McInnes, K , Howard, J., Miles, G. and Crowley, K. (2011) Differences in practitioners' understanding of play and how this influences pedagogy and children's perceptions of Play. *Early Years* 31 (2): 121–33.

Melzer, H., Gatward, R., Goodman, R. and Ford, T. (2000) *Mental Health of Children and Adolescents in Great Britain.* London: The Stationery Office.

Milevsky, A. (2014) Siblings of children with disabilities. *Psychology Today.* www.psychologytoday.com/gb/blog/band-brothers-and-sisters/201406/siblings_

Milton, D.E.M. (2014) So what exactly are autism interventions intervening with? *Good Autism Practice* 15 (2): 6–14.

Mistry, M. and Barnes, D. (2013) The use of Makaton for supporting talk, through play for pupils who have English as an additional language (EAL) in the Foundation Stage. *International Journal of Primary, Elementary and Early Years Education* 6: 603–16.

Mitchell, W. (2008). The role played by grandparents in family support and learning: Considerations for mainstream and special schools. *Support for Learning* 23 (3): 126–135.

Montessori Group (2018) Changes to the Early Years Foundation Stage. www.montessori.org.uk/media/changes-early-years-foundation-stage-eyfs

Montessori.org.uk (n.d.) The philosophy behind the Montessori approach. Montessori.org.uk/about-us/what-is-montessori

Morton, K. (2018) Children's centres facing cull nationwide. *Nursery World*. https://www.nurseryworld.co.uk/News/article/children-s-centres-facing-cull-nationwide

Moss, P. (2006) From children's services, to children's spaces. In: Kay, E., Tidsdall, M., Davis, J.M., Hill, M. and Prout, A. (eds) *Children, Young People and Social Inclusion*. Bristol: The Policy Press.

Moss, P. (2007) Bringing politics into the nursery: Early childhood education as a democratic practice. *European Early Childhood Education Research Journal* 15 (1): 5–20.

Moyles, J. (2015) Starting with play: Taking play seriously. In: Moyles, J. (ed.) *The Excellence of Play*. Maidenhead: McGraw-Hill.

National Autistic Society (2016a) Obsessions, repetitive behaviours and routines. www.autism.org.uk/about/behaviour/obsessions-repetitive-routines.aspx

National Autistic Society (2016b) Sensory differences. www.autism.org.uk/sensory

National Foundation for Educational Research (2007) Getting to grips with moderation. www.nfer.ac.uk

National Health Service (NHS) (2018) Newborn blood spot test – Your pregnancy and baby guide. www.nhs.uk/conditions/pregnancy-and-baby/newborn-screening/

National Portage Association (2019a) Partners with parents and children. www.national-portage association

National Portage Association (2019b) Support for parents. www.portage.org.uk/parents/parent-partnership

National Portage Association (2019c) What is Portage? www.portage.org.uk/about/what-portage

Nelson, F. (2016) The return of eugenics. *The Spectator*. www.spectator.co.uk/2016/04/the-return-of-eugenics/

Nimmo, S. (2019) Significant other. *Woman & Home*, July.

Nunkoosing, K. and Phillips, D. (1999) Supporting families in the early education of children with special needs: The perspectives of Portage home visitors. *European Journal of Special Needs Education* 14 (3): 198–211.

Nutbrown, C. and Clough, P. (2009) Citizenship and inclusion in the early years: Understanding and responding to children's perspectives on 'belonging'. *International Journal of Early Years Education* 17 (3): 191–206.

Nutbrown, C., Clough, P. and Atherton, F. (2013) *Inclusion in the Early Years* (2nd edn). London: Sage.

Office of Head Start (2018) About Head Start. www.acf.hhs.gov/ohs/about

Ofsted (2004) Special educational needs and disability: towards inclusive schools. HMI 2276 London: Ofsted.

Ofsted (2019) Education inspection framework – equality, diversity and inclusion statement. www.gov.uk/ofsted

Orr, R. (2003) *My Right to Play – A Child with Complex Needs*. Maidenhead: Open University Press.

Parliament UK (2019a) Government's SEN reforms failing young people and parents. www.parliament.uk/business/committees/committees-a-z/commons-select/education-committee/news-parliament-2017/send-report-published-19-20/

Parliament UK (2019b) Special educational needs and disability enquiry. www.parliament.uk/business/committees/committees-a-z/commons-select/education-committee/inquiries/parliament-2017/special-educational-needs-and-disability-inquiry-17-19/

Parliament UK (n.d. a) Baroness Warnock. www.parliament.uk/biographies/lords/baroness-warnock/1733

Parliament UK (n.d. b) The Education Act 1918. www.parliament.uk/about/living-heritage/transformingsociety/parliament-and-the-first-world-war/legislation-and-acts-of-war

Parsons, T. (1971) The normal American family. In: Adams, B. and Weirath, T. (eds) *Readings on the Sociology of the Family*. Chicago, IL: Markham, pp. 53–66.

Pellegrini, A. and Blatchford, P. (2002) Time for a break. *The Psychologist* 15 (2): 60–2.

Pen Green (2018) A celebratory approach to SEND assessment in the early years. Available at: https://www.pengreen.org/a-celebratory-approach-to-send-assessment-in-the-early-years/

Pugh, G.A. (2001) Policy for early childhood services. In: Pugh, G. (ed.) *Contemporary Issues in the Early Years* (3rd edn). London: Sage.

Purdue, K. (2009) Barriers to and facilitators of inclusion for children with disabilities in early childhood education. *Contemporary Issues in Early Childhood* 10 (2): 133–143.

Revels, J. (2015) Implementing the Special Educational Needs and Disability Code of Practice 0–25 – opportunities and challenges in equality & inclusion. *Early Education Journal* 75: 7–9.

Rinaldi, C. (2005) Documentation and assessment: What is the relationship? In: Clark, A., Kjorholt, A. and Moss, P. (eds) *Beyond Listening: Children's Perspectives on Early Childhood Services*. Bristol: The Policy Press.

Rix, J. (2011) What's your attitude? Inclusion and early years settings. In: Paige-Smith, A. and Craft, A. (eds) *Developing Reflective Practice in the Early Years* (2nd edn). Maidenhead: Open University Press.

Rix, J., Paige-Smith, A. and Jones, H. (2008) 'Until the cows came home': Issues for early intervention activities? Parental perspectives on the early years learning of their children with Down syndrome. *Contemporary Issues in Early Childhood* 9 (1): 66–77.

Rix, J., Sheehy, K., Fletcher-Campbell, F., Crisp, M. and Harper, A. (2013) Exploring provision for children identified with special educational needs: An international review of policy and practice. *European Journal of Special Needs Education* 28 (4): 375–91.

Roberts, J. (2019) Lack of special educational needs and disability support – failing a generation of pupils. *The Times Educational Supplement*. www.tes.com/news/lack-send-support-failing-generation-pupils

Roberts-Holmes, G. (2015) The datafication of early years pedagogy: 'If the teaching is good, the data should be good and if there's bad teaching, there is bad data'. *Journal of Education Policy* 30 (3): 302–15.

Rochford, D. (2016) *The Rochford Review*. London: Standards and Testing Agency.

Rogoff, B. (2003) *The Cultural Nature of Human Development*. New York: Oxford University Press.

Rose, J. and Rogers, S. (2012) *The Role of the Adult in Early Years Settings*. Maidenhead: McGraw-Hill.

Runswick-Cole, K. (2008) Between a rock and a hard place: Parents' attitudes to the inclusion of children with special educational needs in mainstream and special schools. *British Journal of Special Education* 35 (3): 173–80.

Royal College of Speech and Language Therapists (2019) *Understanding the links between communication and behaviour.* Available at: www.rcslt.org.

Runswick-Cole, K. (2019) How special needs families are finding their voice in SEND battle. www.yorkshirepost.co.uk/news/opinion/columnists/how-special-needs-families

Runswick-Cole, K. and Hodge, N. (2009) Needs or rights? A challenge to the discourse of special education. *British Journal of Special Education* 36 (4): 198–203.

Savage, K. (2015) Children, young people, inclusion and social policy. In: Brodie, K. and Savage, K. (eds) *Inclusion and Early Years Practice.* Abingdon: Routledge.

Save Childhood Movement (n.d.) School readiness. www.toomuchtoosoon.org/school-readiness.html

Save the Children (n.d.) *Early Language Development and Children's Primary School Attainment in English and Maths: New Research Findings.* www.savethechildren.org.uk/content/dam/gb/reports/policy/early-language-development-and-childrens-primary-school-attainment.pdf

Scope (n.d.a) Getting support from and giving support to friends, family and other parents. www.scope.org.uk/advice-and-support/support-to-from-friends-family-parents/

Sellgren, K. (2019) Special needs pupils with care plans 'vulnerable'. www.bbc.co.uk/education-49640713

Sheehy, K. and Duffy, H. (2009) Attitudes to Makaton in the ages of integration and inclusion. *International Journal of Special Education* 24 (2): 91–102.

Shehata, G.A. (2016) Childhood cognitive impairment. *Acta Psychopathologica* 2: 37.

Slee, R. and Allan, J. (2005) *Excluding the Included: A Reconsideration of Inclusive Education.* Abingdon: RoutledgeFalmer.

Smith, C., Reid, J. and Robinson, D. (2018) Special educational needs and inclusion: Policy and practice. In: Johnston, J. Nahmad-Williams, L., Oates, R. and Wood, V. (eds) *Early Childhood Studies – Principles and Practice.* Abingdon: Routledge.

Standards and Testing Agency (2018) National Curriculum assessments – Key Stage 1. *Pre-key stage 1: Pupils working below the National Curriculum assessment standard.* https://www.gov.uk/government/organisations/standards-and-testing-agency

Stone, L. (1977) *The Family, Sex and Marriage in England 1500–1800.* London: Weidenfeld and Nicolson.

Sunstein, C. (2017) *#Republic: Divided Democracy in the Age of Social Media.* Princeton, NJ and Oxford: Princeton University Press.

Sure Start (2005) Birth to Three Matters. Sure Start. https://www.foundationyears.org.uk/wp-content/uploads/2012/04/Birth-to-Three-Matters-Booklet.pdf

Sutton-Smith, B. (2003) Play as a parody of emotional vulnerability. In: Roopnarine, J. (ed.) *Play and Educational Theory and Practice, Play and Culture Studies.* Westport: Praeger.

Swain, J and Cook, T. (2005) In the name of inclusion: 'We all, at the end of the day, have the needs of children at heart'. In: Rix, J., Simmons, K., Nind, M. and Sheehy, K. (eds) *Policy and Power in Inclusive Education – Values into Practice.* London: RoutledgeFalmer.

The Guardian (2017) Sally Phillips' film on Down's is 'unhelpful' for families warns ante-natal specialist. www.theguardian.com/society/2016/oct/01/downs-syndrome-screening-jane--fisher-expert-criticises-sally-phillips-bbc-documentary

The National Archive (2003) *Together from the Start – Practical Guidance for Professionals Working with Disabled Children.* webarchive.nationalarchives.gov.uk/20130402161029/https://www.education.gov.uk/publications/standard/publicationDetail/Page1/LEA/0067/2003

Thompson, G.A., Shanahan, E.J. and Gordon, I. (2019) The role of music-based parent-child play activities in supporting social engagement with children on the autism spectrum: A content analysis of parent interviews. *Nordic Journal of Music Therapy* 28 (2): 108–30.

Thompson, P. (2019) Supporting play. In: Fitzgerald, D. and Maconochie, E. (eds) *Early Childhood Studies – A Student's Guide*. London: Sage.

Tomlinson, S. (1982) *A Sociology of Special Education*. Oxfordshire: Routledge.

Tutt, R. and Williams, P. (2015) *The SEND Code of Practice 0–25 Years – Policy, Provision and Practice*. London: Sage.

United Nations Educational, Scientific and Cultural Organization (UNESCO) (1994) The Salamanca Statement and Framework for Action on Special Educational Needs. *Ministry of Education and Science, Spain*. www.unesco.org/education/pdf/SALAMA

United Nations International Children's Emergency Fund (UNICEF) (1989) The United Nation's Convention on the Rights of the Child. www.unicef.org.uk/what-we-do/un-convention-child-rights/

University of Leicester (2015) The social and medical model of disability. www2.le.ac.uk/offices/accessability/staff/accessabilitytutors/information-for-accessability-tutors/the-social-and-medical-model-of-disability

University of Michigan (2009) Siblings of kids with special needs. www.med.umich.edu/yourchild/topics/specneed.htm

University of Oxford (n.d.) Grandparents contribute to children's wellbeing. www.ox.ac.uk/research/research-impact/grandparents-contribute-childrens-wellbeing

Volf, M. (1996) *Exclusion and Embrace: A Theological Exploration of Identity, Otherness and Reconciliation*. Nashville, TN: Abingdon Press.

Waitoller, F.R. and Artiles, A.J. (2013) A decade of professional development research for inclusive education: A critical review and notes for a research program. *Review of Educational Research* 83 (3): 319–56.

Ward, U. (2010) *Working with Parents in Early Years Settings*. Exeter: Learning Matters.

Warnock, M. (1978 [2005]) Warnock U turn on special schools. *The Telegraph*. www.telegraph.co.uk/news/uknews/1491679/Warnock-U-turn-on-special-schools.html

Weale, S. (2019) Support for children with SEND in crisis. *The Guardian*. www.theguardian.com/education/2019/oct/04/support-for-children-with-special-educational-needs-in-crisis

Weale, S. and McIntyre, N. (2018) 'Special needs pupils being failed by system on verge of crisis'. www.theguardian.com/education/2018/oct/22/special-needs-pupils-being-faile....

Weinberger, J., Pickstone, C. and Hannon, P. (eds) (2005) *Learning form Sure Start – Working with Young Children and Their Families*. Maidenhead: Open University Press.

Weisberg, D.S., Zosh, J.M., Hirsh-Pasek, K. and Golinkoff, R.M. (2013) Talking it up – Play, language development, and the role of adult support. *American Journal of Play* 6 (1): 39–54.

White, C. (2017) *The Label – A Story for Families*. Brighton: MENCAP.

Wilkinson, M. (2015) Education, schools and universities: Policies of the political parties. *The Telegraph*. https://www.telegraph.co.uk/news/general-election-2015/114/4579/education-policies.html

Wolfendale, S. (1993) *Assessing Special Educational Needs*. London: Bloomsbury.

Wright, J., Williams, R. and Wilkinson, J. (1998) The development and importance of health needs assessments. *British Medical Journal* 316 (7140): 1310–13.

www.parliament (DU) 1918 Education Act. https://www.parliament.uk/about/living-heritage/transformingsociety/parliament-and-the-first-world-war/legislation-and-acts-of-war/education-act-1918/

YouGov (2019) Exploring the issue of off-rolling. On behalf of Ofsted. https://www.gov.uk/government/publications/off-rolling-exploring-the-issue

INDEX